DYKE IDEAS

SUNY Series, Feminist Philosophy
Jeffner Allen, editor

DYKE IDEAS

PROCESS, POLITICS, DAILY LIFE

JOYCE TREBILCOT

STATE UNIVERSITY OF NEW YORK PRESS

Published by
State University of New York Press, Albany

For information, address State University of New York Press,
State University Plaza, Albany, N.Y., 12246

Production by Marilyn P. Semerad
Marketing by Theresa A. Swierzowski
Text and cover design by Lou Robinson

Library of Congress Cataloging-in-Publication Data

Trebilcot, Joyce.
    Dyke ideas : process, politics, daily life / Joyce Trebilcot.
      p.   cm. — (Suny series, feminist philosophy)
    ISBN 0-7914-1893-6 (acid-free paper). — ISBN 0-7914-1894-4 (pbk.
: acid-free paper)
    1. Feminist theory. 2. Lesbianism. 3. Radicalism. I. Title.
II. Series.
HQ1190.T74 1994
305.42'01—dc20   93-31712
                                                                          CIP

10 9 8 7 6 5 4 3 2 1

CONTENTS

Preface..*vii*

MYSTERY

Notes on the Meaning of Life.......................................3
"Craziness" 11

GUILT

The Prick/Chick...19
Guilt 21
Stalking Guilt...23
Dissecting Guilt..29
Story 39

PROCESS

Dyke Methods 43
Ethics of Method 59
Not Lesbian Philosophy..67

COMPETITION

Competition..79
Envy 87

SEX

Taking Responsibility for Sexuality 97

Hortense and Gladys on Sex 111

Decentering Sex..117

VALUE

Lesbian Feminism in Process 127

On the Edge 137

Notes on Words 143

Acknowledgements 149

PREFACE

Each writing in *Dyke Ideas* springs from puzzlement or pain or hope. Why do I behave as I do? Why do I have a particular belief or value? Why, on some subjects, are some lesbians so different from me? Must I go on feeling like this? I write also to connect with wimmin, to find wimmin like me, to learn about wimmin who are like me and those who are different; to be known by wimmin; to get attention. I write in the hope of contributing to wimmin's cultures, of helping to make some wimmin's lives better, including my own. When I was working fulltime as a professor, I wrote also for money (raises were said to be based mainly on publications) and for respect among academics.

Dyke Ideas reflects both my dyke values and my academic training as a philosopher in the analytic and positivist traditions. In that training, a scholar was defined as a "truth-seeker," one whose task is to discover not mere opinion but what is true for everyone. I was taught to make generalizations based on evidence and then to defend them from counterexamples. I was taught to focus on trying to say something that everyone would have to accept, that no one could find persuasive reasons against. I was taught that my purpose should be to be "right." Only later did I realize that I was being trained to participate in the construction and maintenance of a system that coerces belief.

Now I choose not to focus on what is "universally true," but to speak only for myself. If parts of what I say are interesting or helpful to others, I suppose that is not so much because they are "true" as because they interpret or suggest or remind or inspire in ways that fit into the work of other wimmin who, like me, are engaged in making accounts of their worlds. Unlike the professional philosopher I was trained to be, I do not (consciously) try to get others to agree with me. Both attempting to speak for others and trying to get them to accept my ideas as their own strengthen the hierarchical systems in which experts have power over those they define as ignorant, in which rich white males have—attempt to have—power over everyone else.

My approach to writing about an idea is not so much to give definitions, which is often at the center of analytic philosophizing, but to try to figure out where I got the idea in the first place. I am interested in sources because I believe that I am more likely to have control—to end the puzzlement or pain— if I know where an idea comes from. The exploration of sources is partly a matter of articulating and evaluating the reasons I have for a particular belief or value. It includes also a consideration of feelings that motivate me to accept those reasons, and of the settings in which the feelings occur.

Some of my ideas have come to me from my experiences of being a member of a patriarchal category of oppressors or oppressed, and I want to be aware of these political sources, not just of the (sometimes seemingly "unbiased") reasons they provide. The oppressor groups I belong to include "american," white, middle-class, thin, relatively able, california-raised, of christian background (catechism classes from the catholic church as a child). The oppressed groups include female, old, and "homosexual." (Before the Second Wave, I was heterosexual.) Both sorts of categories provide experiences that instill specific values and beliefs; (the system is designed so that many—most?—of those experiences are forgotten by those who have them).

During the decade or so I worked on these writings I became more and more aware of the likely influence of now-forgotten experiences in my past on my ideas and behavior and of the importance of exploring these connections. This approach is an application of the classic feminist principle that the personal is political. It is used in my work in stark conflict with the method in which beliefs and values are supposed to be primarily products of reason and perhaps even also of certain feelings (e.g., empathy), but certainly not of experiences that might be (but sometimes except for detail only seem to be, as consciousness raising reveals) peculiar to a particular individual. I still have much to learn about how my ideas have grown from my particular background—my memory contains lots of blanks and even with memories, connections between the past and present are difficult—but I believe that comprehending ideas, one's own and others', importantly involves knowing where they come from psychologically as well as logically (in terms of reasons) and politically (in terms of oppressions).

I believe also that some of wimmin's experiences of suffering—in rape, beatings, humiliation, poverty, illness, loneliness—can not only help to illuminate later ideas and behavior but can also be clear windows into the workings of male domination. In the spirit of making lemonade out of lemons, I say that rather than being "damaged" and so not to be taken seriously, wimmin who have been hurt in oppressive systems may have especially lucid ideas of how oppressions operate as, for example, many incest survivors do.

I want these writings to be as widely accessible as I can make them and still say what's on my mind. I would like wimmin who are bored or offended by academic writing, wimmin who don't much like to read, wimmin without much education, to grasp my meanings if they are interested. The relative absence of the jargon, gratuitous complexities, and esoteric references characteristic of much academic writing may limit the fun for some readers—I myself have sometimes enjoyed material because I knew it was difficult and challenging and required a special and hard-to-acquire background. But an elitist style is pleasurable mainly for those who want to be part of an elite.[1]

---

[1] For comments on some of the ways I use language, consult "Notes on Words," pages 143-48. Discussion of the spellings "wimmin" and "womon" begins on page 147.

For a while I wanted this book to be titled "In Process" to convey that I am permanently engaged in figuring out what's going on and what to do and that I reserve the right to change in any or all respects. But then I decided on "Dyke Ideas" in order to say that my way of thinking/feeling is intimately connected with being a dyke, which for me means having radical lesbian feminist ideals, including the following:

Being alert to and active against oppressions;
Taking every womon seriously, especially by attending
    to what each womon has to say; and
Empowering wimmin in contexts that wimmin create.

MYSTERY

Notes on the Meaning of Life

Coming of age in the Beat context of Berkeley in the fifties, influenced by existentialism and full of angst, I accepted readily the idea that I would have to make meanings for myself. I would sometimes say that I had nothing to do with my life except whatever was "best"; my plan was to figure out the best thing to do and and then do it. The quest went on for decades. This writing reports one aspect of it.

(Readers who may be distressed by portrayal of male sexuality may wish to skip this piece.)

Most women live most of the time defending ourselves from environments that are pervasively phallic. Not only are we constantly warding off actual fucking, rape, molestation, and harassment, we are also subject to ubiquitous images of looming and lurching phalluses. Even scholarly essays refer to issues arising, points to be made, penetrating analyses, hard cases, thrusts, and upshots (while analyses judged to be inferior may be said to be "all wet and full of holes.")

I became especially conscious of the omnipresence of phallic culture when I discovered that I had devoted a great deal of my best energy over a period of years to a problem that was a problem for me only because I had failed to realize that its form was determined by male sexuality. I had been trying to apply to my own life values that men had derived from their sexual experience, clearly a doomed project.

THE TWO ETHICS

In the male-dominated groups of mainly young, white, intellectuals and artists that I hung out with before feminism, two sorts of values were openly advocated: ecstatic experience and extraordinary achievement. I came to think of these as "the experience ethic" and "the achievement ethic." The former extols mystical joy: the illumination, the experience of merging and oneness, that may come through practices such as meditation, fasting, and drug-taking; sustained and focused sex; the making of art or contemplation of nature; and so on. Such experiences are sought for their own sake and sometimes also for the psychic and physical powers that may be associated with them. Despite their dangers ("merging" can make one crazy), such extraordinary experiences are often presented as the best that life has to offer. When I was in college, for example, in literature and philosophy and even science classes I was overwhelmed with tales of awesome experiences had by "great" men, and with the message that seeking and having such experiences makes for a truly "superior" life.

The achievement ethic focuses on great works or deeds that are valued partly for their own sake, for the satisfaction of accomplishment, but mainly as means to fame, money, and power. And immortality. Immortality here does not mean perpetual existence as an individual consciousness but, rather, continuing attention to one's works or deeds, and hence oneself, even after one's death. In this ethic, the idea is for works and deeds to have far-reaching influence in terms of both the people affected and the length of time that the influence continues, and one's name should be permanently attached; but an anonymous contribution that lasts even a short time after one's death is taken as better than none at all. (The quality of a contribution tends not to enter into the equation insofar as a crime or an atrocity brings the same rewards as a work of art or heroism.)

Before I had much comprehension of how these values worked, I began to read, think about, and experiment with them. I had rejected the values I was expected to adhere to—particularly marriage and motherhood—early on as boring, stifling, intolerable; I needed to be independent and unencumbered. So I turned away from the values imposed on females of my time and place and race and class and turned instead to those designed for men.

Understanding these values, experience and achievement, as two separate and competing systems, I thought I had to give priority to one or the other. But extraordinary experience meant pushing myself physically and emotionally, staying awake for days, seeking always the bizarre, the incongruous, the perfectly beautiful: whippets racing across a vast lawn in the fog at dawn. Achievement, on the other hand, meant having an address, being able to get up at least some mornings, working longer and harder and smarter than those I was competing with (it meant competition, which I participated in avidly but hated). It seemed clear to me that the two sets of values were incompatible.

Yet I was attracted to both. The logical purity of the ecstasy ethic seduced me: it made perfect sense to me, trained as I was in individualism, that what one sought ultimately should be a state of consciousness, and that that state of consciousness should have *intrinsic* value, should be an end in itself. The achievement ethic seemed more muddled: what, after all, was one after? Immortality was clearly a fraud, since one would be dead when it happened, and what was the point of fame and money and power? These must themselves be means to some further ends. Less theoretically, I liked the lifestyle of the experience ethic ("All experiences are worthwhile," I used to say and believe; only years later did I begin to add an "except" clause). Also, the ideology of ecstatic experience promised discipline—and justification—for my emotions, which were often chaotic. On the other hand, I needed the self-esteem that accomplishment could provide. And I liked the work—it was and is deeply exciting to me to make something that I think is worthwhile. I was also attracted by the prospect of immortality, although I felt a bit guilty about it. (I felt *more* guilty about my desire for fame, money, and power and so did not admit even to myself that I wanted them; they were definitive of the dominant culture that had to be rejected.)

Sometimes I shifted back and forth between the two ethics, going to school, for example, with wholehearted concentration and academic success, and then dropping out so I could live without a schedule. Or, during another period, I alternated between three or four days of writing poetry (with a bit of part-time work for money) and then three or four days with my friends, plunged into emotional and physical intensity. Later, when I was in a job as an assistant professor that seemed to demand that all of my energy be devoted to achievement, as part of my attempt to achieve I wrote an essay in which I argued, against the philosophical establishment, that it is not irrational to "live for the moment," thus realizing an isolated synthesis of the two ethics.[1]

THE SEXUAL CONNECTION

I have come to appreciate that the form of the two ethics is the form of male sexuality, that is, of male orgasm and reproduction. For men, transcendent experience is associated with orgasm, and immortal achievement with impregnation.

I need hardly argue for a link between orgasm and ecstatic experience: orgasm *is* (supposed to be) ecstatic experience.[2] Patriarchal psychologist Abraham Maslow calls attention to the link in the context of a discussion of what he calls "the peak experience," noting that some of his subjects (who were overwhelmingly male) give accounts of their mystical experiences in terms that are also used to describe orgasms:

There were the same feelings of limitless horizons opening up to the vision, the feeling of being simulta-

---

[1] "Aprudentialism," *American Philosophical Quarterly* 11, no. 3 (July 1974): 203-10.

[2] Of course not everyone finds ecstasy desirable.

neously more powerful and also more helpless than one ever was before, the feeling of great ecstasy and wonder and awe, the loss of placing in time and space with, finally, the conviction that something extremely important and valuable had happened, so that the subject is to some extent transformed and strengthened even in his daily life by such experiences.[3]

As ecstatic experience is associated by men with orgasm, so impregnation is taken by them to be an achievement. A classic example from patriarchal literature is provided by Diotima, when, in Plato's *Symposium*, she speaks explicitly from a male perspective and asks:

Who, when he thinks of Homer and Hesiod and other great poets, would not rather have their children than ordinary human ones? Who would not emulate them in the creation of children such as theirs, which have preserved their memory and given them everlasting glory? . . . [A]nd many others there are in many other places . . . who have given to the world many notable works, and have been the parents of virtue of every kind; and many temples have been raised in their honor for the sake of children such as theirs. . . .[4]

When I understood that men associate intense experience with their orgasms and immortal achievement with their giv-

---

[3] Abraham M. Maslow, *Motivation and Personality*, second edition (New York: Harper and Row, 1954), 164. I take Maslow's account to be propaganda designed to get people so focused on sex that we don't have time or energy to change the social and political structures that control us.

[4] Plato, "Symposium," in *The Dialogues of Plato*, translated by B. Jowett (New York: Random House, 1982, 1920), marginal number 209, 333-4. Jerome Schiller, a scholar of classical Greek philosophy, read this piece (it was part of a dossier I submitted for a promotion I did not get); he suggests that I would do better to refer to Plotinus here because Plotinus—but not Plato—says clearly that "in contemplation, we produce."

ing genetic material to a baby, the conflict I had felt between
the two value systems began to dissolve: in the male imagi-
nation, I realized, orgasm in intercourse and the impregnation
of a woman are *one and the same event*: for at least many men, to
have an orgasm in a woman's vagina is—ideally, "naturally"—
to impregnate her. (Hence, many men reject contraception
because for them, at a gut level, it stymies not only their capacity to reproduce but also their very orgasms.)

For women, in contrast, orgasm and pregnancy are *independent*. Indeed, in contemporary u.s. society, it is likely that
female orgasm is only occasionally a precursor to pregnancy;
most episodes of heterosexual activity evidently do not include
female orgasm at all.[5] For women, reproduction is emphati-
cally *not* a matter of having an orgasm which, even if it occurs
on the occasion of impregnation, is as nothing compared to
nine months of pregnancy and childbirth: surely it is these,
along with the raising of children, that constitute reproduction for women.

This difference explains why men find no conflict between
the two ethics, but I do. For men, it is obvious that through
ecstatic orgasm one creates babies, and through other experiences that break through the usual limits of personality one
may create great art and science and heroism. For them, spew-
ing forth seed is *both* ecstasy *and* creation of a new reality. For
me, orgasm was not at all connected with *achievement*. And
reproduction was certainly not connected with any kind of positive experience, for I had been pregnant in high school and
had an illegal abortion. While men intuitively identified orgasm
with reproduction and so ecstasy with creation, such connections for me were at best abstract and weak. For men there was
but one integrated system: orgasms produced the next generation. For me, the two values were in conflict. The conflict
plagued me because I didn't notice that the values I was struggling with were men's, designed by and for men, and I did not

---

[5] Shere Hite, *The Hite Report: A Nationwide Study of Female Sexuality* (New
York: Dell, 1976), especially the chapter on intercourse.

realize that men's values cannot be authentic for me.

Once I began thinking about the two ethics as projections of male sexuality and therefore as not applicable to me, my problem with them disappeared. I stopped trying to choose between them. And by then I had developed other kinds of values. I had become more aware of the lousy lives most women live in patriarchy and had begun to make changing the conditions of our lives a central concern. I realized that I did not, after all, like either of the two values I had been struggling over: "merging" frightened me because it makes one vulnerable, and achievement angered me because it is competitive. Both, I came to think, are promulgated in hierarchical culture to keep people from paying attention to what is really going on. True power is reserved for only a few, so others must be kept occupied with individualistically seeking the elusive rewards of ecstasy and immortality.

As I began to think in this way, I became more and more clearly aware that what moves me most deeply is not sex or ecstatic experience, not reproduction or achievement, but wimmin, the worldwide movements of wimmin.

I thank Fox (then Jeanette Silveira), Claudia Card, and Julien S. Murphy for suggestions about this essay.

"Craziness"

What I used to call my craziness started many years ago, when I was in my late twenties. I devoted several years almost entirely to it, deliberately moving into the experience, trying to get through the fear, trying to figure out what to do to get through it. Finally, I gave up. I had tried everything, nothing worked; there was, I thought, something deeply, maybe permanently, wrong with me. So I gradually learned to avoid the occasions of craziness and turned my attention to other things—especially, to graduate school. But, for years, I had the sense that this problem, the problem of my craziness, had to be dealt with, that it would be a great tragedy for me—a great personal defeat—to die without dealing with it.

The core experience was auditory. There were two stages. First, intrusion. Men—male voices—would overhear my thoughts and want to get in. But they didn't want simply to be there, they wanted control. There was something they wanted to make me do. They would scream "Talk! Talk!" and I would be unable (as I thought then) to do what they wanted or (as I thought later) I would refuse to do it. This, then, was the source of the craziness—invasion and control, and the threat of invasion and control.

The emotions I had were, first, anger, rebelliousness: "I won't do it and you can't make me." Surrounding and interlarding the "you can't make me" response were fear—terror that I would lose, lose the fight, lose control, lose my self—

and self-hatred and guilt that I couldn't do what I thought they wanted, what I thought I should do. There was also embarrassment that my "inferiority" (what I thought of as my inferiority) was so obvious. And I felt a terrible frustration, despair, that I could not figure it out, that I did not know what to do, how to change.

All this constituted what I called the craziness. The heart of it was the anger (madness), the "you can't make me" response, primarily as it occurred at the point between penetration and control. The heart of it was the defiance, the resistance to being controlled, the angry, desperate preservation of a core, a kernel of privacy and self-direction. I *had* to protect this kernel, this separate self.

Usually, when I was into the experience of craziness, every person I met, every voice I heard, wanted to invade me, wanted me to talk. I remember writing a long poem once about the voice on the recording that gives the time over the telephone; I thought she knew about me, and I was terrified. I experienced everyone as mocking me, ridiculing me, hating me because I wouldn't let them in or wouldn't let them control me. I was in almost continuous emotional turmoil. I cried a lot, and ran through the streets sobbing, and punished myself, and traveled, moving repeatedly to new places in order to try again with new groups of people. And I would smoke a lot of dope, and try different drugs, getting high over and over, trying to break through, trying to cross over, trying to move into and remain in a different consciousness; doing so seemed to me to be the most important, the only, thing worth doing. I kept trying to think about how to do it, to figure out how to do it.

When I was not in the experience, I thought that some of what I heard was projection and some was not, but I did not develop the ability to tell the difference. Doris Lessing suggests a criterion for differentiating:

> *There are different qualities in thought. . . . Very slight differences in quality. . . . Remember this, remember it. Words*

trickling through your head with no emotion: that's likely to be overheard, someone else's thought. There is emotion in the self-hater.[1]

There is, then, a difference in the quality of what is heard: a toneless voice, as in reading, versus the virulent inflections of the self-hater. I did not learn to make this distinction.

Consciously, I was drawn to the experience because of the lightness and power of participation. My early values— acquired primarily in Berkeley during the beat time as a street person and student—made participating in "ecstatic communion," whether through drugs or religion or art or sex or some other means, a high and consuming priority. I consciously accepted this value but nevertheless I would regularly block when it seemed that magical shared experience was imminent.

Class may also have been a factor in my single-minded longing for transcendence. As the only child of parents who were barely high school graduates, I was, I think, especially susceptible to elitist values. Early on I believed that the experience I was trying so desperately to have was the province of only a privileged few: those visited by grace or the muse, the talented, the disciplined, the ones who made sacrifices. I was determined to join them: I thought I should be able to do anything if only I tried hard enough, an attitude typical of the powerless. Later, when I came to believe that "anyone"— except me—could do it on drugs, simply by getting high, I was desperately confused.

My resistance to—shall I call it "merging"?—has roots far back in my history. Long before I was aware of hearing the voices of men trying to rape me, I resisted being controlled by my mother. To cite just one example, my mother points out that I was rather late in learning to talk, but that when I did talk, whole sentences, even paragraphs, came out. What was happening, as she and I both understand it now, is that my

---

[1] Doris Lessing, *The Four-Gated City* (New York: Bantam, 1969, 1970), 537 (emphasis in original).

refusing to talk was a way of my resisting her control of me. Mother wanted the baby to speak, but the baby wouldn't do it. Later I wouldn't say what men wanted me to. Later still, as an academic, I had writing blocks; I would refuse to write and publish philosophy papers in order to show that I could survive, even as an academic, without doing what they wanted me to do. I now understand all these refusals as resistances to rape, that is, to invasion and control by others.

My interpretation of these experiences has shifted over the years. In early feminism, when I first began to think that what I called my craziness was connected to patriarchy, I believed that all the rapists were male and that I could overcome the craziness by separating from men and being with women. Later, I realized that while the self-hater was certainly male and, sometimes, women had spoken to me in male voices, I had also been threatened by women as women. Simply choosing women is no protection against having words put in one's mouth.

I also shifted away from self-blame. At the most painful time, it seemed to me that what was going on was that I wanted to do what they wanted me to do, that I wanted to participate in what was going on, but I simply could not, I was unable, I did not know how. I had the sense that there was a trick to it, something I had to learn. I now think that this non-participation was not inability, but refusal: it was not that I could not take part, but that I would not. And the reason I would not was in order to protect myself from the assault, from the intrusion, from the loss of my own will. So I think now that while I at that time experienced myself as being unable to do something I wanted to do, I was in fact taking good care of myself. I resisted in order to continue as an individual—in order not to be submerged, subjected, merged.

The patriarchal term "crazy" applies to all this, first, because I was certainly behaving in ways some patriarchal cultures take to be typical of craziness—raving and crying. Also, when I talked about what was happening to me, my talk was "crazy talk." And I expect that the conflict itself—between seeking and resisting psychic touching—counts as crazy, although there is not much discussion of that in patriarchy. One who quietly merges is not crazy, and one who refuses isn't either. The craziness is to keep putting yourself in the middle of the conflict, which is what I kept doing, in the hope of getting through it. (Later, of course, I learned to avoid the conflict, and for years now I've mostly stayed away from it.)

My deep-seated tendency to resist the rapist, to resist penetration, was for me a preparation for separatism. My experience of patriarchal psychic merging as rape and, in particular, my exercising tremendous energies to resist it (have I said that it was not easy to be high, psychically naked, surrounded by people trying to connect with me, fending them off by building up cement-block walls?)—this work was practice, as it were, for the work that separatism requires. As I then refused to submit to men, so, as a lesbian separatist, my work now is to refuse to submit not only to men but also to men's values. As I then was constantly vigilant to keep men from reading my mind (but I did not always succeed), so now I am constantly vigilant to keep patriarchal values out of me (but I do not always succeed).

I do not mean to suggest that separatism precludes my having the experiences I call craziness. The intrusive voices, the conflict, the screaming and crying can all happen in separatist space as in patriarchy. There is some difference though. Lesbian separatists, I believe, are likely to be respectful, even supportive, of craziness—the kind I have described here and other kinds as well. A womon feeling crazy is less likely to be rejected among dykes than among men.

GUILT

The Prick/Chick

I

Suppose every word you write is designed (by some deep swish designer) to punish yourself, a part of the self-hate deep within (and then right here on the skin too, scars from picked pimples) so the work has the patina of real work but is never quite authentic, never quite complete, cryptic, touches but fails to analyze the deeper questions because you're a bad girl and don't deserve more.
The situation feeds on itself. Self-hate breeds self-hate.
How can I like the dyke who does this to herself? Oh, lovingly, gently, caressingly.
Oh fun and games. A slow smile.
Oh seriously.
The resources of the motive to defeat myself seem endless.
Self-hate is a prick within me sapping my best energies, twisting skillfully my every effort.
The chick within.
Made by him, is him, to constantly defeat me.

II

Is there some way to suddenly strangle him, the prick/chick? (And take on the murder rap for more guilt?) Or will he, she, it wither and die of neglect? Or separatism: how can I separate from what is within? Or the discipline of art: will insistence upon completeness, detail, authenticity ultimately drown him? (Surely not: he invented art.)

Perhaps naming the prick/chick
and laying it out in the cold

Perhaps changing the rules
for what counts as success

Perhaps not having success at all,
or stardom or self-importance.

Politics is for the purpose, ultimately, of sitting on the beach. When Shulamith Firestone went to the Sufi convent, we thought that a fine statement.

Desperately.

Calm. What is the value of sitting on the beach if doing so doesn't feed politics or art? Doesn't touch someone else, doesn't last? (All those ideas are from the prick/chick.)

Guilt

Guilt is self-punishment.
Gnawing one's own arm is
The ultimate sin.

My mother says
I want to hurt her.

I hide from the cops
in a house with a cat.

I stole thousands of dollars once
to give the guilt a peg
and pay the rent.

My mother wants
to control me.

I regret nothing,
and constantly flee capture.

Stalking Guilt

I

At what moment of girlhood did I decide to foil my mother and myself? To be neither me nor whom she wanted me to be? Was it in that last moment of the birthing—last moment of solitude, independence—before she claimed me hers and I recoiled, shrinking back even then, to a quiet, floating, musing state of my own, my own—?

Or was it later? When she left me in the crib crying, screaming with anger because, on doctor's orders, she did not pick me up? I was lonely and determined to survive; I learned to be lonely.

Or was it still later, when it became clear to me that Angela, the mother, had nothing to do but care for him, her husband, and me, the only child—nothing in her life but being a good wife and mother, which meant that she deeply needed me to be what the neighbors admired?

II

How did it happen that I not only put misery in her life but in my own as well? How did it happen that I find myself now, at the second Saturn return, her dying in another city and me with sand in my mouth and palpitations and fantasies of leaving, quitting, closing up, going away, abandoning my most unsatisfactory world? How did it happen? Did I simply decide that since I could not, would not, be what she wanted, I could not be what *I* wanted either? Was my life the price for spoiling hers?

III

I search for a new memory that will tell me. A child, a girl, decided to fight parental power. Daddy was always smiling in the background. He liked to see us opposed, females in conflict are reassuring to men. Did I fight mother to please him? Erotically position myself as independent, sexual, a scholar—versus my mother the homemaker—with him, smiling, in the background? I cried no tears when he died. "What a relief," I thought.

IV

It won't be long now until Angela, the mother, dies too. Then I will be entirely relieved of the burden of parents. I will have no living relatives. I have longed for that. To be in the womb again. Alone, where they can't get to me.

V

Is there no way out from duty? For surely it is my duty to suffer in payment for what I have done to Angela: the illegal abortion in high school that she and my father had to arrange—forty years later she still keeps bringing it up with horror and sorrow, to her it is the central fact of my life; my refusal of marriage, of motherhood, and even, for many years, refusal to have a regular job—which made me incomprehensible to her; drugs; poetry; escaping the U.S., living as far away as I could get (the U.S. of the fifties, who would not escape if she could?); a crime, prison—. Do I really believe that even now I must pay for all of this, pay for Angela's pain, by not doing what I want? By being blocked, isolated, immobile?

VI

Or is all this a cover for some lack in me? A manuscript sits on the shelf and I cannot finish it because I do not want it, do not want those ideas scoffed at by wimmin. (No, I made that up, that's not central.) Because I am tired, can't sleep, can't write, can't handle being afraid of an earthquake coming and needing to rearrange my books and all the distractions I invent so as not to get on with this work wherein I make no progress but just keep reliving the same images.

VII

So now I say no more memory. I have already remembered all the memories. A new approach. Enveloped in envy of other writers, unable/unwilling to talk with men, isolated in my room above the New Madrid fault, I rush through these words without tears, wanting to get to the conclusion, the explanation, the solution, to understanding.

To be able to work. To let Angela die. To forgive. "I forgive you for all you did, Angela, mother," does not ring true. "I forgive you, Joyce," to myself, is not true either.

VIII

I hold Angela responsible because she was older, because she was the mother, because she was supposed to understand what was going on and know what she was doing. But she was tied up in her woman's deprivation and narcissism. She had no idea of her place in the world. She had very little courage. Her life consisted of a man, a child, a house.

I cannot forgive her for not rebelling. Why didn't she go out and do something for herself besides taking that course on Japanese flower-arranging? Why didn't she even have a friend?

IX

But I want to reject patriarchy, to reject men's system of guilt and morality and rules and good and bad rather than to forgive her or myself within the system. To forgive is to play by the boys' rules. Still, if forgiving is a way of getting rid of guilt—

X

Angela was so much a part of that system that SHE WAS TRYING TO MAKE ME FEEL GUILTY. Of course. That's obvious, my mother *wanted* me to feel guilty for not being the daughter who would make her life make sense to her.

What she wanted from me, if she couldn't control my daily life—and she couldn't—was guilt. She wanted me guilty. All those things I did, the travel and adventure—she thought were terrible things done deliberately to hurt her but to me they were exciting, done partly for me and partly to show her my freedom. She insisted that I either conform or feel guilty. She wanted me to feel guilty.

I am amazed by this idea because I have not yet purged myself of the image of her that she worked so hard to create, the image of the *good* mother, the *kind* mother, the *benevolent* mother—the very same mother who was working so hard to make me feel guilty. She wanted me guilty. And still does.

That desire was imposed on her by the system in which she had her being: men's reality, men's values, patriarchy. Patriarchy caused my pain and hers.

What a surprise.

XI

To get free of this connection with Angela. I will not forgive her nor refuse to forgive her. Rather, I will comprehend that we were two females made by men in *their* interests. I will make now, even at this late time, a clean separation—like a bear cub who takes nourishment from her mother but then goes off on her own, and neither child nor mother expects more of the relationship. I will remember that the family is a primary mechanism of pain in patriarchy.

Dissecting Guilt

I want immunity from guilt. I want immunity from guilt because guilt means pain but also because through guilt I do the patriarch's work for him. Through guilt I control my own behavior according to his rules: I punish myself for wanting success and hence have only partial and pale success; I punish myself for wanting power and so remain closed up; I punish myself for failing to fulfill an image he has created of me and so I get fat or drunk or squeeze pimples on my face (or so I used to do). In addition, through guilt I collaborate with arrogant and powerful males who make me feel so inferior that I am eager for any crumb of identity and hence fall easily into pretending my own "superiority" as white, educated, older— whatever seems to boost me a bit—thus helping to impose guilt on others.

I am furious that men have made me do this cruel work for them, and sad for what I and other wimmin might have been and done otherwise.

I want wimmin immune from guilt when we must deal with patriarchy, and free from guilt—with no occasions for guilt, not even concepts of guilt—in the spaces we make for ourselves.

ON HOW GUILT HELPS MEN

To feel guilty, as I define the term here, is to want to hurt oneself because, one believes, one *deserves* to suffer. A woman who feels guilty punishes herself in large and small ways, often without awareness that she is doing so. Her punishment means that she should feel bad, so she denies herself access to and expression of her authentic self/selves. In full-blown guilt, she collaborates with the patriarchs around her by cranking up self-hate and by arranging to have trouble in her worldly dealings, by setting up rejections, losses, failures. For poignancy, she may allow herself to get just to the verge of some success—and then spoil it. For continuity, she may repeat the patterns of her most effective—most painful—self-punishments over and over, even for an entire lifetime, even taking some satisfaction in that idea.

Ruling men construct guilt and impose it on those they choose to oppress, but the particular punishments one who feels guilty undergoes are decided by the victim. Thus, a woman who feels guilty, trapped by men's demand that she punish herself, denies herself whatever she longs for most—a decent place to live, a certain work, a particular relationship or capacity. Because each woman knows intimately and exactly what she most seriously wants and, hence, what is most painfully denied her, each woman is the perfect punishing mistress for herself. Given the aims of men, guilt is a brilliant invention.

Feeling guilty not only means punishing oneself, it also nourishes *conscience*, which I take to be forward-looking guilt (fear of guilt/punishment in the future) and thus a motive for continuing to obey the oppressors' rules. Conscience moves me to conform to values other people want me to have not because I have examined and adopted them as my own but because I want to escape pain. I don't simply refuse to engage in self-punishment because the feelings of guilt are usually so overwhelming that I can't think clearly and also because the mechanisms of guilt are (therefore) largely unconscious. Thus, when guilt is working, it not only turns me into an instrument of my own denial of my self/selves through self-punishment, it also makes me enforce my own obedience to systems of imposed values by motivating me to avoid future guilt. In these ways, oppressors use guilt to make us do their work for them: we administer punishments to ourselves, and struggle to conform to values that are not our own and are harmful to us, all in the service of keeping rich white men in power over us.

ON SOME FORMS OF GUILT

In thinking about how patriarchs use guilt to do their work for them, I have distinguished some familiar kinds of guilt.

Identity Guilt

What I here call identity guilt is implied by definitions of persons that are imposed and hence oppressive: women as defined by men, lesbians as defined by heterosexuals, people of color as defined by whites, fat people as defined by non-fat people, etc. Such definitions not only stereotype and degrade those on whom they are imposed, they also, paradoxically, both blame the oppressed for being who we are, thus suggesting that we have the power to change, and imply we have *no* power because our condition is innate and immutable. For example, a traditional patriarchal definition of white women includes the claim that we lack courage. I respond to this put-down with the idea that courage is something one can acquire. So I grit my teeth and put myself in challenging situations; I practice courage. But in patriarchy I am still treated as a white woman, as one who is timid and fearful, so I blame myself for not being able to become courageous. So I feel guilty, and am inclined to punish myself. For those with traditional concepts of women, however, my lack of courage is part of my immutable nature; it makes no sense for me to try to change because nothing I can do can make me okay. And so in identity guilt I am inclined to keep punishing myself for failing to escape from an imposed stereotype, even though I "know" that I am permanently trapped in the "inferiority" of my supposed identity.

When, in this kind of situation, I am inclined to punish myself, I do so, it seems, with both reformist and retributivist intentions. I punish myself partly in the hope of making change: if being as I am leads consistently to enough hurt, I will be *forced*, I think, to change, to get "better." But I also have an idea of retribution: I feel that punishment is required not only in order to change me but also just because I "deserve" it, just because of my "badness."

The same treatment that creates identity guilt also instills shame, a useful partner of guilt from the patriarchs' point of view. While effective guilt moves its victim to self-punishment, shame moves her to hide herself, to cooperate with the patriarchal task of making her invisible—of making *her* invisible, leaving in her place a shell, a puppet, a robot, although even that vestige is treated as though it doesn't exist if it is not pleasing enough to men. Through guilt, dominators try to tell the subjugated that we are so bad that we must harm ourselves. Through shame, they try to tell us that we are so offensive, so disgusting, that we must crawl off in a corner and disappear. Guilt and shame are central to the creation of the identities of the oppressed.

Victim's Guilt. That my very identity as decided by heteropatriarchs means that I must be perpetually in a state of guilt and shame is taught to me partly through my being raped, beaten, impoverished, made to take orders, spit upon, invisibilized. Through such treatment I am supposed to understand not only that I am "inferior" in my most fundamental nature but also—and here is an additional layer of guilt—that through some specific selfishness or stupidity I have caused each attack and insult I have suffered. So not only am I intended to hate myself essentially, for being who I am, I am also intended to hate myself over what I said or did or wore or thought on each particular occasion that the message of my "inferiority" is hammered into me.

Two important outcomes of this treatment from the standpoint of the oppressors are that I am super-motivated to try to please them (even knowing I cannot) and I am busy-busy-busy trying to escape them, trying to please them, and punishing myself—too busy and too battered, they hope, to get calm and get organized and get guts enough to effectively resist.

Oppressor's guilt. Even in the midst of my own oppression there are pressures upon me to feel superior to others—as white, middle-class, able-bodied, older than the young and younger than the old, and so on. These pressures come in part from my own oppression, from the desperate need for self-esteem it creates in me. I am not supposed to be aware of my role as *both* oppressor and oppressed. In some environments, however—for example, in white feminist organizations where anti-racism work is done—that most people are participating in the oppression of others is made explicit and is the object of at least verbal resistance. In such settings, oppressors are likely to feel guilty about their collaboration with oppression and so to focus on themselves, on self-punishment, rather than on changing the systems of oppression. It is in the interest of those on top that when oppressors begin to become aware of our collaboration with the system, we get stuck in guilt about that, which intensifies our preoccupation with ourselves and further weakens our capacity for meaningful resistance.

Guilt about guilt. Guilt can pile up in meta-levels until some people—mainly women—are encrusted in layers and layers of it. Feeling guilty—being inclined to punish oneself—is of course "bad," one is not supposed to want to hurt oneself, so one feels guilty about that; that higher-level guilt in turn is reason for further guilt; and so on. Once the process begins, guilt is secreted continuously—unless the victim herself puts a stop to it.

Official Guilt

What I call official or polite guilt stems from some *particular* violation of laws or rules (*not* from who one is) and belongs to legal and moral systems that provide for its elimination: one is (found) guilty, takes one's punishment, and that's the end of it—the guilt, which is mainly a matter of *being* guilty rather than *feeling* guilty—is designed to be temporary. Also, the specific punishment is prescribed and administered primarily by official representatives of the system, not by the guilty themselves. Shame has no role in this sort of guilt, for an officially guilty person is expected to stand up "like a man," not to cover himself and hide. I call this guilt polite as well as official because it is part of recognized moral/legal systems, studied and defended by mainstream intellectuals, and acknowledged in polite society; unlike identity guilt, it is a fit subject of dinner-party conversation in the homes of the powerful.

Official guilt differs from identity guilt most strikingly with respect to the role of retribution. An analogy with marketplaces is relevant here. In a market, a monetary price is paid in exchange for some commodity. In guilt, punishment is the price paid in exchange for the elimination of the guilt. In official guilt, as in a market, the price, once agreed upon, is specific and finite. But in identity guilt, the punishment is not like a market price but like endless extortion. Because identity guilt is primarily a matter of who one is (of who one is supposed to be), no payment short of death can ever be enough to end it; strictly speaking, no payment is possible, yet we who suffer such guilt flagellate ourselves endlessly in futile attempts to pay off our debt and/or to transform ourselves into something more acceptable. It is as though we imagine that we are in a rational system where we can be tried and convicted and sentenced and then work off our debt to society—but we've been tricked, we're not in that sort of system at all. In polite guilt, peers are reunited with peers after a period of estrangement; in the guilt of oppression, those who impose the guilt and those who suffer it are not and never can be peers.

Forgiveness is another part of the guilt system that is supposed to provide a means for reconciliation between the guilty and those from whom they are estranged. It works only for official guilt, not for identity guilt. In official guilt, forgiveness signals the commitment of the once-guilty person to conform to the violated rule and to renounce whatever spirit of resistance may be buried in the guilt; it also marks the willingness of those responsible for the banishment to readmit the perpetrator to their community. In identity guilt, forgiveness is impossible because a person who feels identity guilt has done no wrong. In the case of a survivor of child abuse, for example, the survivor may forgive an abuser and so free him or her from official guilt, but no one can "forgive" the survivor for having been (defined by others as) "bad" and "worthless." The survivor felt guilty, but was not in fact guilty of anything.

I regard forgiveness with suspicion because it is designed to mend breeches in established communities, whereas I always hope for new forms of being together. Often, especially when it is rebelliousness (rather than, for example, thoughtlessness) that leads to an occasion for forgiveness, I hope that the rule-breaking spirit will be followed away from an existing community instead of being renounced.

FEMINISTS FOR GUILT

As I have been thinking and talking about guilt I have been astounded to learn that some of my lesbian feminist friends *like* guilt—they think it's useful, and don't at all share my commitment to be rid of it. I want to give their ideas some attention here.

One womon tells me that she values guilt because when connections among friends are broken by some offense, guilt provides a way to mend them. As I understand her idea, it is that if I have avoidably done something that hurts you, and if I feel terrible because of it, my pain restores the balance between us, makes us "equal" again, because we both will have undergone similar suffering. If I *don't* feel guilty for hurting you, if I allow you to be in pain because of what I have done without imposing similar pain on myself, I put myself in a dominant position over you, thus precluding the possibility of friendship. According to this opinion, if I care about you as a peer and if I am responsible for having harmed you, then I must punish myself.

My objection to this arrangement is, of course, that it creates pain: one womon has been hurt, and therefore there must be more hurting. So I want to know how wimmin can respond when one has avoidably hurt the other *without* using guilt. Imagine that you and I care about one another and then I harm you in some way that I could have avoided, and so you're angry. One possibility is that we have come to the end of our relationship. It is not, after all, an imperative that all broken relationships be mended. Patriarchs need cohesive, closely knit communities for ease of control, but dykes do not. We can just let broken relationships end—there are other wimmin for each of us to be with.

On the other hand, suppose we both want to heal the relationship. You still care about me, so you may want to understand why I acted as I did and want me to talk to you about it, and I may be willing to do so. I still care about you, so I may try to stop your hurt, to fix it, to take care of you in some way, and you may be willing to accept my help. With such talking and nurturing, we may mend our friendship, without guilt or forgiveness. I do not feel guilty, which is to say that I don't judge myself deserving of punishment, and you do not forgive me, which is to say that you do not place yourself in the position of making a moral judgment about what I did. (Notice that in this analysis I have stepped onto the path that leads from guilt to morality, to the whole web of moral concepts. I am not going to follow that path here except to remark that of course rejecting guilt means rejecting at least much of the structure [not necessarily the substance] of morality, and to add that this is a consequence I welcome.)

Other friends of mine who want to retain the possibility of guilt point out that it can help one to adhere to values that one has consciously chosen but that are difficult to conform to, that is, to one's own ideals. One woman says that she values guilt because it motivates her to be more active politically. In particular, she feels guilty about not doing more to oppose certain actions of the u.s. government abroad, and she thinks that this guilt inspires her to go to meetings, make phone calls, write letters, and so on. Strictly speaking, the motivator here is conscience, the desire to avoid guilt: my friend establishes a rule for herself and is determined to suffer if she doesn't follow it, so wanting to avoid the suffering helps her obey her rule. A similar example was mentioned to me by another womon who thinks that her guilt about sneaking cigarettes is helping her to break her smoking addiction. When she smokes, she tells me, she hates herself, so to escape that punishment—she hopes—she will stop smoking entirely.

Each of these wimmin thinks that guilt is the best choice as a motivator for her, as a way of overcoming the forces that are blocking her from doing what she is committed to do. But such forces—laziness, fear, self-hate, habits—may be foiled by determination, courage, strength, solidarity with others, and so on. Guilt is not the only way to push oneself to be who one wants to be. So why choose guilt?

I have said that I want immunity from the guilts imposed in patriarchy and that I want ways of interacting with wimmin without guilt. I also have the task of exorcising guilts already in me: finding and confronting them, hanging on to them, observing them work rather than numbly being worked over by them. This task, as I comprehend it, is of a piece with other anti-hierarchist work. Guilt is connected with morality is connected with power is connected with ranking is connected with competition is connected with buying and selling is connected with violence is connected with the thigh bone. Some say it gives us something to do.

Thanks for ideas to Barbara Flagg, Magda Mueller, Ryn Edwards, Sandra Bartky, and Victoria M. Davion.

Story

I have always resented my mother
for trying to control me

But maybe it wasn't my mother but
my father

Trying to control me
A "thumb" at a peculiar angle
between my legs

Feeling tingly

And then being abandoned
screaming and screaming

mouth open wide, flat out

PROCESS

Dyke Methods

First Principle:	**I speak only for myself.**
Second Principle:	**I do not try to get other wimmin to accept my beliefs in place of their own.**
Third Principle:	**There is no given.**

The methods I discuss here are, most narrowly conceived, methods for using language. They are, therefore, methods for a great deal else as well—experiencing, thinking, acting. But my focus is on language, on verbal language, on english; my focus is on how, as a dyke—a conscious, committed, political lesbian—I can use words to contribute to the discovery/creation of consciously lesbian realities.

The center of this writing is the statement of three principles. I dislike the term "principle" for its air of arrogance, its association with fixed rules and judgments. Nevertheless, I have decided to use this word because I have no better brief name for a belief or value that is not just one among many but applies over a wide range of thought and action. So I say that these values are principles, but I stress that they are not rules: *The three principles are not rules to be followed.* I do not intend them to be adhered to by others and I can "violate" them myself if I want to at any time without guilt.

Sources of the Principles in My Experience

The principles come mainly from anger, from anger about being controlled.

This control is exercised by men (and male-identified women) over women/wimmin and girls of their own or a subordinated race and class in a variety of ways, of which—as I have learned through feminism—two of the most effective are erasure and false naming. In erasure, men make us invisible either by claiming that we are included when we are not (as in terms such as "mankind") or by simply ignoring us; in false naming, they define us and then impose their definitions upon us (as in their concept of woman).

Another manifestation of control by men is that women/wimmin adopt the very means of oppression that the dominators use, and apply those techniques against ourselves and one another. For example, I have been in the audience of sessions of the Society for Women in Philosophy and of the National Women's Studies Association when lesbian feminist speakers have made claims about wimmin, about dykes, about "we," that erase or misdescribe me. In such cases, if I maintain my sense of who I am, I am excluded; if I feel myself a part of the "we" being discussed, I distort who I am. This difficulty is not only mine; I have heard other wimmin say that the misuse of "we" in lesbian and feminist settings is hurtful for them as well.

But long before feminism, I was angry because of attempts—often successful—to control me. My earliest experience of being controlled was as the only child of a distant and narrow-minded father and a domineering mother who, with single-minded dedication, attempted to make me what she wanted me to be. I was also controlled, of course—and in certain respects still am—by institutions designed by powerful white men to keep people in line: christianity, heterosexuality, academe, capitalism, and so on.

These and similar institutions participate in what I sometimes call the truth industries—heteropatriarchal science, religion, scholarship, education, media—which are used by men to formulate, preserve, and exercise their power. In dominant culture "truths" are presented as claims that people are required to accept as bases for their thinking and action and hence identities, regardless of how *they* feel about the "truths" and regardless of their relevant experiences. By means of the apparatuses of "truth," "knowledge," "science," "revelation," "faith," etc. (it matters little whether the methodology is scientific or religious), men are able not only to project their personalities as reality, but also to require that other people participate in those realities and accept them as their own. Recipients of the "truth" (i.e., all those not certified to create it) are expected to long for truth, to respect it, to bow down to it, and, especially, to honor—and obey—those who are authorities on it. The system is thoroughly corrupt; it hurts me, angers me, and, when I have my wits about me, strikes me as silly. How ridiculous, for example, for men to go on an archeological dig and report that what they have found is what is there, when I would come back with quite a different story were I to dig, and other wimmin would come back with yet other stories. I am trying to find ways of writing without imposing my "truths"—the analyses and values that are meaningful to me— on other wimmin. The three principles I explicate here help me in this process.

Where the Principles Apply

My life is like a murky river with some clear pools and rivulets—wimmin's spaces—but most waters thick with the sludge and stink of patriarchy. The principles I discuss here belong to the (relatively) clear waters.

They are not intended to be used in situations that are predominantly patriarchal, that is, when getting something from men is at stake, as when one is working in patriarchy for money or political concessions, doing business with men and male-identified women, etc. In these contexts, I find that it is often most effective—that is, on the whole more helpful than harmful to wimmin/women—to proceed according to patriarchal ideas of knowledge and truth.

When both patriarchal and feminist elements have a significant part in a situation, the principles do apply, although in

ways limited by patriarchal power. Women's studies classes
sometimes have this character; sometimes, for example, for a
class to work, both in relation to the institution and in relation
to the students in it, the teacher must operate partly with patriarchal principles and partly as a co-discoverer/creator of wimmin's spaces.

In situations that are predominantly wimmin-identified,
in contrast, I want to throw off mainstream habits and values
in favor of the more direct and diverse patterns of wimmin. I
should add that, for me, patriarchy is always present: there is
no "pure" wimmin's space. (As if in compensation, when wimmin are present there is no pure patriarchy—we are always
violating and sabotaging it.)

THE PRINCIPLES

First Principle: I SPEAK ONLY FOR MYSELF

I speak "only for myself" not in the sense that only I am my
intended audience but, rather, in the sense that I intend my
words to express only my own ideas about the world. I expect
that some wimmin will find that what I say is more or less
true for them too and that some will not. (And that in both
groups, some will find my ideas to be useful to them, and others will not.) I want to assume differences and to learn to leave
spaces for them.

Let me give an example of how the idea that I speak only
for myself works. Suppose I am inclined to write "We all
need love." Because I wish to speak only for myself and
thereby to acknowledge the likelihood that there are wimmin who do not believe that *they* need love, I refrain from
the plural "we." There are several alternatives. First, instead
of "We all need love," I may write "I need love and some
other wimmin report that they also need love." This social
science sort of approach presupposes data—written or verbal
avowals from other wimmin. In what I would take to be
appropriate scholarship, the wimmin who are reported on

have themselves authorized the use of their words in the context in question; they themselves participate, as it were as co-authors, in the work. With this approach to fulfilling the principle that I write only for myself, feminist scholarship moves in the direction of becoming collective scholarship, a not surprising outcome.

A second way of reacting to the inclination to write "We all need love" in a way consistent with speaking only for oneself is to write instead something like "I need love and it seems to me that some other wimmin also need love"; or perhaps, "My image of wimmin is that we all need love." In formulations like these I remind myself and my audience that I am talking about only my own beliefs, concepts, definitions, imagings—and that I am leaving space for accounts by others, especially by the wimmin I am describing, whether or not those accounts are significantly different from mine. With this approach I remind the reader that when I am writing about other wimmin, the distinction between my opinion and other wimmin's is (even when the opinions themselves are identical) methodologically significant.

The third and perhaps best alternative is that, in place of "We all need love," I write simply, "I need love." If I choose this approach, I clearly speak only for myself, and so attach my theorizings—that is, whatever explications, explanations, predictions, or proposals I may connect to the claim that I need love—clearly and closely to my self, in accordance with the feminist belief that the personal is essentially involved in both knowledge and liberation.

I have said that I intend my words to express only my own ideas. But my ideas are formed partly by men. Hence, in speaking for my self, often—to my horror, when I realize it—I am speaking also for men, for patriarchy. For example, when I, a white woman, speak in racist ways, I express white men's racism as well as my own. Part of the process of becoming able to speak only for my chosen dyke self is to become more aware of oppressive ways of thinking and speaking and to change them.

Second Principle: I DO NOT TRY TO GET OTHER WIMMIN TO ACCEPT MY BELIEFS IN PLACE OF THEIR OWN

The first principle, that I speak only for myself, suggests the second, that in talking about my beliefs I reject the purpose of trying to bring it about that other wimmin substitute my beliefs for their own. I sometimes call this the principle of nonpersuasion. In this context, the term "persuasion" must be construed broadly so as to include not only argument and discussion but also other forms of deliberately influencing people's beliefs, such as emotional manipulation of various kinds.

Of course the principle of nonpersuasion does not preclude my telling other wimmin what my beliefs and values are, and I may certainly give them information, whether of a particular and perhaps trivial sort (e.g., "I'll be there at ten-thirty") or, for example, information I might relate to a class about herstory or feminist theory. The principle of nonpersuasion holds that I should not try to mold wimmin's minds, not that I should not give them information and ideas that they can use, if they choose, in making up their own minds, in making up their own realities.

Not trying to get other wimmin to accept my ideas in place of their own is a principle primarily about intention rather than about behavior. Whether a particular kind of behavior counts as persuasion varies from situation to situation and among cultures, so there is no kind of behavior that is always precluded by the principle. Indeed, I find that applying the principle does not require much change in how I act—I can still set out my convictions and my reasons for them (as I do, for example, here). But my attitude changes—it no longer includes the intention to persuade, an intention to which I became habituated in patriarchy.

Despite my rejection of persuasion, wimmin may, of course, be influenced by me to adopt as their own some of my beliefs, even though those beliefs are not authentic for them; this is especially likely in situations in which I am perceived as having higher status. The principle of nonpersuasion cannot and does not require that I in fact do not cause other wimmin to believe in certain ways, but only that I refrain from trying to do so.

This principle, then, takes seriously the cliché that everyone should think for herself. In patriarchal scholarship, this notion is likely to be presented against a background image of "a marketplace of ideas" where many producers present their wares, hawking them with arguments, competing with one another for attention and allegiance, and consumers buy some ideas but not others. The principle that in making a statement I do not try to get others to accept it suggests not an image of such a marketplace but one of a potluck: we each contribute something and thereby create a whole meal. It is understood that our contributions may be diverse and may seem, on some standards, not to go well together, but we are not bothered by that; we each choose according to our own taste, eating from our own and/or other dishes. The food I bring is usually something I like myself, but also I want to share it—I hope that at least some others will like it too.

In writing dyke philosophy it is important to me that someone else thinks that at least some of my work is worthwhile. But I want my work to be used by other wimmin because they find it helpful in terms of their own experiences, not because I have persuaded them, however gently, that what I say is true. I wish to learn to present my work not as ideas for sale in a competitive marketplace but as fruits to be shared with those who are so inclined.

Third Principle: THERE IS NO GIVEN

This principle, like the second, is suggested by the first. Not only do I speak only for myself but, ultimately and in principle, *only* I speak for myself. That is, the task of discovering/creating reality requires in the long run the exploration of every facet of existence through my feminist lesbian consciousness. In principle, I need to rewrite for myself the entire world as patriarchy has presented it to me. In practice, a finite lifetime and the call of other amusements make doing so impossible. Further, other dykes are doing some of the work, and in many cases I can integrate their analyses into my own. Still, the principle that there is no given reminds me that at every step I need to consider how patriarchal assumptions may be distorting who I am and what I think, leading me back into the service of men.

The claim that there is no given does *not* mean that there is no oppression, that men don't give us plenty to struggle against. I understand that for most females (including me, much of the time), daily life is experienced as replete with givens, with phenomena imposed from the outside; I do not mean to deny the reality of rapists or racism or poverty, for example, or of the baby crying in the next room. In saying that there is no given, I mean, rather, that every patriarchal assumption, every axiom of received reality, is ultimately to be questioned for the purpose of deciding whether to accept it as it is, change it, or reject it entirely: all the alleged immutables of nature, of the human condition, of ultimate reality, must be identified and evaluated.

Consider how controlling and pervasive patriarchal givens are. For example, in writing about wimmin's lives, part of the background of my discussion is the many assumptions shared by me and my readers about the necessary conditions of human life—that, for example, humans and hence wimmin must have food and water and air to survive; that our lives generally last less than a hundred years; that we are subject to pain; and so on. When these topics are not themselves the subjects of my discourse, I am likely, as a matter of habit and convenience, to accept such assumptions not merely as true but as givens in the sense that I take them to be immutable, to be written into the nature of things. And, indeed, they are written into the nature of things—but not by me, nor, yet, by any womon. So they are "givens" only on sufferance: temporarily and, even then, suspect.

The idea that there is no given means not just that every "given" needs to be reexamined in dyke consciousnesses, but also that dyke consciousnesses may define reality in such a way that there are no givens at all, that is, no "nature" (or deity), no immutable facts of nature (or metaphysics) that wimmin are forced to accept and build upon. In developing ideas in one area it may be helpful or even necessary to assume a fixed background of as-it-were immutable conditions, but these may be understood as assumptions for the sake of discussion and further creation/discovery rather than as facts of nature. The principle that there is no given not only calls attention to the need to question the assumptions and presuppositions of a particular focus, it also is a reminder that many familiar conceptual schemes that require givens are designed by privileged men in their own interests.

QUERIES AND REPLIES

In this section I address what seem to me to be the most important objections and puzzles inspired by the three principles. These are organized as three queries: the query about persuasion, the query about community, and the query about pie-in-the-sky.

Query About Persuasion

Probably the most serious worry I have about what I have written so far has to do with the second principle, which is that I do not try to get other wimmin to accept my beliefs as their own. I have two concerns about this claim. First, it is not true: I sometimes do try to persuade others. Second, and more important, I wonder whether it ought to be true: surely there are situations in which I *should* try to get others to agree with me.

Reply to the first part. Yes, I often do try to persuade others to accept what I say as their own. Sometimes I do this for the fun of arguing and sometimes I do it out of moral and political conviction. In some of the situations in which I try to persuade others to adopt my views, resisting the temptation to attempt to persuade would be appropriate but, rather than resist, I act out of old habits. All three of the principles are ideals, and I do not always live up to them. On other occasions, however, the principle of nonpersuasion does not apply because the situation is patriarchal; these principles, as I have already said, are designed for wimmin's spaces.

But part of what constitutes wimmin's space is the exercise of these principles. That is, wimmin's space is defined partly by ways wimmin treat one another; the intended absence of conceptual/intellectual hegemony or, more broadly, serious respect for differences among wimmin, which is the point of the principle of nonpersuasion, is one of the characteristics of wimmin's space. Thus, there is an intimate relationship between acting in accordance with the second principle (and, indeed, with all three of the principles I have articulated here, as well as others) and the nature of the space one is in. I define whether a space or situation is wimmin's partly in terms of whether the principles I am discussing here apply; conversely, whether the principles apply depends on whether the space is wimmin's.

Consider a case in which I am a teacher in a women's studies classroom in a mainstream university. If the classroom situation is very patriarchal—a large beginning class of fifty or sixty students, say, with few feminist students—I am likely to define my task as largely one of recruitment and so to find persuasion—for example, persuading students that women are oppressed—an essential tool. I do not follow the principle against persuasion, which does not apply here. In contrast, in a smaller and more advanced class, I may enter into the exploration of the ideas of a student where these ideas run counter to my own, not with the prospect of her beliefs changing but, rather, with the intention of participating in the articulation of those beliefs. By acting in accordance with the principle of nonpersuasion, I contribute to the creation of wimmin's space in this classroom.

Reply to the second part. The second part of the query about persuasion urges that in wimmin's spaces there sometimes are situations in which I *should* try to persuade others to accept my beliefs as their own. This idea is based on the conviction that some beliefs are so harmful that changing them, or trying to change them, is more important than avoiding the imposition of one's own beliefs on others.

My understanding of such situations is that they are defined by patriarchal values and so are not wimmin's spaces. Imagine, for example, a group of women/wimmin in which a white woman says something racist. I want her to be quiet, to take it back, not to talk like that, and I tell her that I have these wants, and why. So far, I have acted consistently with the second principle. I have told her how I feel and what I think about her words, but I have not asked her to cease her racist talk nor argued that she should do so.

In fact, of course, my telling her my reaction to her words may function as a sanction, so that she may change her behavior and even her beliefs in order to please me—but this response, which is part of the traditional female role of acting according to the wishes of others, is her responsibility, not mine. On the other hand, the womon may consider my words on their own merits, without regard to her relationship to me, and decide in the light of what she has heard that she wants to change. In the former case, I persuade despite my intention not to; in the latter, I do not persuade, but the womon nevertheless changes.

But suppose that the woman who makes the racist remarks continues speaking in a racist way despite my telling her that I hear her words as racist. If she agrees that they are racist but doesn't care, the space we are in is not wimmin's (in wimmin's spaces oppression is repudiated), and I may either withdraw or, acknowledging that the situation is patriarchal, try to persuade her to change. On the other hand, if she disagrees about *whether* her words are racist, claiming that they are not, we may together explore the question, each giving an account of our interpretation. In neither case do I go against the second principle.

Query About Community

Feminism, especially lesbian feminism, is essentially based on "we," on communities of wimmin conscious of ourselves as wimmin moving together against patriarchy. But in my emphasis on difference, perhaps I obliterate community; in my emphasis on multiplicity, perhaps I obliterate solidarity.

Another way of formulating this concern is to ask whether there must not be something that all feminists, or all dykes, agree on, whereby we are all entitled to be called "feminist" or "dyke." Surely being a dyke, while partly a matter of action and style, is also partly a matter of having certain beliefs. Perhaps more important, it is essential for wimmin to have shared beliefs as a basis for politics, so that we may stand together in strength against patriarchy. The query that emerges from these considerations is whether the principles I articulate here, while protecting differences among wimmin, sacrifice our being together as wimmin (as those who focus on community might say) or our acting together against capitalist heteropatriarchy (as those who emphasize political action might say).

Reply. Communities of wimmin are wimmin acting, speaking, thinking, singing, playing, feeling, not necessarily the same but in concert, together. The three principles imply that I will not try to bring this about by persuading wimmin to accept some set of beliefs, but they do not prevent my participating in and encouraging community. The principles preclude my imposing a "we" on others, but they do not mean that wimmin cannot share values and beliefs and self-definitions; they do not mean that wimmin cannot move together, thus creating a "we."

More explicitly, while being a dyke is in part to have certain beliefs—for example, belief in the creative power of wimmin—being a dyke is also, I think, to come to these beliefs oneself, not to internalize them in reaction to someone else's intention that one do so. Of course, wimmin generally learn dyke beliefs partly from one another—indeed, community consists partly in this interaction. But learning from one another does not require the intention to persuade. Nor does sharing beliefs presuppose persuasion. Dyke communities, where wimmin share some central beliefs and values, may come into being without persuasion, through wimmin defining and redefining ourselves in interaction with one another.

In my experience, groups of dykes often form because wimmin have sought each other out, wanting to be with others with similar ideas. Such groups sometimes then decide to act together in political contexts on the basis of beliefs that all the wimmin hold. Having come to these beliefs through observation, interaction, and discussion, they find that they share a solid basis for political action, without anyone having tried to get them to agree.

I want to add that although I try to refrain from acting so as to get other wimmin to adopt the principles I articulate here, I would *like* other wimmin to adopt them. I like to be with wimmin where no one is imposing her views and there is no competition about who has the truth. When wimmin who share my anti-hierarchical, anti-competitive values get together, we tend not to argue or to try to persuade, but to tell our stories—past, present, and future, actual and fantastical— and to make plans. In these situations it seems to me that the stories are likely to be comprehended and enjoyed and the plans carried out effectively even though no one is trying to persuade anyone else. Because of these experiences, I do not, as I have said, think that abandoning the purpose of getting others to adopt one's own beliefs lessens community or solidarity; on the contrary, it seems to me that such restraint can strengthen wimmin's sense of shared convictions and commitments.

Finally, I should note that as I use these principles of dyke method, they do not imply that other wimmin should not act as leaders and persuade wimmin to accept *their* beliefs and values. I do not universalize the principles. My purpose is to announce my own (perhaps temporary) adoption of them, not to try to persuade others to accept them.

Query About Pie-in-the-Sky

Assuming a somewhat scolding and definitely pragmatic voice, I say to myself: Joyce, there you go off again, all by yourself, to some imaginary dyke heaven where each woman speaks only for herself, we love one another's differences, and not even nature limits us. I understand that this tendency comes from your separatist heart, but you are wasting your energies. Pure wimmin's spaces can't exist—we are interfused everywhere with patriarchy—and, anyway, we need to be dealing with patriarchal reality now, for they are truly out to get us.

Reply. First, a semantic point: pure wimmin's spaces can't exist in that when they do, the word "wimmin" itself will not be part of them, for despite the spelling, that word refers back to patriarchy; in pure wimmin's spaces, patriarchy is inconceivable. (It does not follow, however, that "pure wimmin's spaces" [with the quotation marks] cannot exist.)

As to the central concern of the query, the need to confront patriarchy: the anger from which the theorizing in this essay comes is like a two-headed snake, one head attacking patriarchy directly (and often in patriarchy's own terms), the other slithering its way *through* patriarchy, making its own spaces, pushing aside men and their products, eliminating patriarchy from its path. Thus, the principles for discovering/creating wimmin's spaces do not preclude attacking patriarchy in its own arena. Indeed, commitment to wimmin's spaces is in fact often conjoined with a commitment to defend and support wimmin/women who are being harmed by patriarchy. In particular, some separatists are regular organizers of and participants in actions that involve confronting men. Moreover, the development of wimmin's spaces may itself lead wimmin to decide on direct political action, as, for instance, in the case of an academic, fired because her research is about separatism, who then chooses to confront the university directly in a campaign to get her job back. It is a mistake to suppose that devotion to wimmin's spaces means that a womon can not or does not engage in political actions against patriarchy.

The methods discussed here are dyke methods because the heart of dykism, as I experience it, is not a matter of sex but rather of rejecting and separating from patriarchy and joining in solidarity with wimmin—a movement to which these principles contribute. One who consciously and on political grounds adopts them thereby participates in dyke process. (It is men, of course, who make sex the center of lesbianism, as they make sex the center of every female identity.)

As what I have already said indicates, my main motive (as far as I know) for developing these dyke methods is one that has always been at the center of my life: that others not control me. My logic here is in part like that of the pacifist who responds to violent treatment with a refusal to be violent in return. I respond to domination with a commitment to discover/create spaces in which domination cannot exist. But unlike the pacifist, who renounces all violence, I do not renounce all attempts to persuade: rather, I sometimes use the master's methods within the master's house for the sake of wimmin/women; in wimmin's spaces, however, I abjure those methods. The principles discussed here may seem an unacceptable renunciation of power to some wimmin. For me, however, they feel empowering: they embody my deepest values.

I appreciate contributions to the content of this essay by Anne Waters, Claudia Card, Jacquelyn N. Zita, Janneke van der Ros, Fox, Jeffner Allen, Julia Penelope, Kim Hall, María Lugones, Marilyn Frye, Ryn Edwards, and Sarah Lucia Hoagland. Also, the writing of Liz Stanley and Sue Wise in their book Breaking Out: Feminist Consciousness and Feminist Research *(London: Routledge and Kegan Paul, 1983) was important to the early stages of the writing.*

For additional discussion of these ideas, see Jacquelyn N. Zita's commentary, "Lesbian Angels and Other Matters," and my response, "More Dyke Methods," in Hypatia *5, no. 2 (Spring 1990): 133-44.*

After I presented a version of "Dyke Methods" at a session of the Midwest Society for Women in Philosophy in the fall of 1986, Sarah Lucia Hoagland sent me a copy of an earlier essay in which Sally Miller Gearhart develops an idea closely related to part of what I say here. Sally Gearhart's thesis is that "any intent to persuade is an act of violence." Her essay is "The Womanization of Rhetoric," in Women's Studies International Quarterly *2 (1979): 195-201.*

Ethics of Method:
Greasing the Machine and Telling Stories

This essay was my response to an invitation to write something for an anthology on feminist ethics. I do not ordinarily use the concept of ethics in my work because it suggests support for dykes making moral judgments not just about men and patriarchy, which is not a problem for me, but about one another, which doesn't fit with my sense of how I want to live. Even so, I couldn't resist the opportunity to connect method and ethics, and so I wrote this piece.

I remember a dim, panelled office at an eastern college. It was my first philosophy teaching job and I would often stay late after classes talking with a colleague, an ambitious young male assistant professor. I was struggling to finish my dissertation, so late one winter afternoon he told me about his own, completed several years earlier: "I spent lots of pages," he said, "on motivation." A shock went through me. Motivation! Could this be someone who understood, someone who shared my obsession about which topics were worth studying and why?

But my excitement dissipated as I came to understand that by "motivation" this man meant merely the reasons why his problem was significant for the development of theory, not for him personally. The dissertation pages he referred to as about "motivation" discussed philosophical, not personal, difficulties that gave rise to the problem he studied. In contrast, motivation for me was a matter of how a particular issue was connected with who I am and who I want to be—a matter of why *I* should be working on this topic. Motivation for my colleague was just about theories; for me, it was about my relationships to theories. This distinction was based, I think, on the fact that my colleague accepted without question or much consciousness an array of values presupposed by the theoretical framework within which philosophy in that time and place was done, while I was uncomfortable with those values (they were, after all, made to fit him and not me), and I needed to articulate and examine them.

I was not able to even begin doing so until a few years later, when feminist ideas were first being developed in academe. Now, in the context of lesbian and feminist thought, I continue to be concerned with values presupposed by doing theory and with motives for working on a particular issue in a particular way. I am interested not only in my own motives but also in those of other writers: why does a feminist choose some topics and approaches and not others?

THE MACHINE

The ideology of dominant western (white, male, capitalist) culture is like a huge and complex machine that requires continual oiling and fixing, continual attention from hundreds of workers whose job it is to maintain and repair the machine and to keep it adjusted to changes and challenges from both within and without. Academics (those academics who are mainly researchers and writers rather than teachers) are trained and supported by society to do the technical work required to keep the machine running.

These maintenance jobs usually provide a moderately good salary, some prestige in mainstream culture, and relatively comfortable working conditions. They offer also the possibility of projecting parts of one's own personality into reality.

That is, an academic may develop a bit of theory that actually becomes part of the general ideology, at least for a while. Although this sort of immortality is rare, its promise, I think, keeps many scholars and researchers at what is often tedious, boring work.

In addition, academics often engage in conventional scholarship because they sense, more or less consciously, that the machine they tinker with, whether or not they actually contribute parts to it, operates in their interest. In the u.s., these academics are white, upper- and middle-class men and those who identify with them (including a few women and men of color and a few white women). Although these academics know that, and to some extent how, the machine benefits them, most do not say that it does, even to themselves, because to notice would be to admit that there are others whose interests it does not serve.

Thus, those who work on the machine tend not to write about motivation in the sense that interests me, that is, by describing their personal, experiential, evaluative connections with their topics. For most of them, as for my early colleague whose mention of motivation I excitedly misinterpreted, the motivation for studying a particular problem is not, or at least not consciously, a matter of making a fit between one's own values and reality.

STORIES

But what about those who are mashed to pieces by the big machine? We are inclined, I think, to articulate into reality ways of thinking, acting, feeling—ways of being—that make real our experiences or that do the same for others who are excluded from dominant ideologies. Inspiration for such work comes, I believe, from a need for authentic accounts of the selves and worlds that the machine is designed to mash.

The issues lesbian feminists choose to work on often come out of our particular experiences, from our particular places in society, from our sense of relationships with other women. An incest survivor may analyze the family; a Chicana may write about the barrio; a white woman may examine racism. Sometimes in such writings the author's motivation is clear even without specific focus on it. Sometimes—I especially like this approach—the author gives explicit account of the particular aspects of her life and values that lead her to make the theory she presents.

In this sort of writing, there need be no pretense that what is said is "universally" or "objectively" true. An author may present her own story as one of many possible and actual stories—other women are likely to have different accounts, and so is she, in different circumstances—and different accounts have different values. Some stories tell a woman who reads or hears them that she is not alone; some give directions or clues for making change; some offer new ideas or information; some give inspiration for action. Some such accounts may be of value only to the author, as a stepping stone from which to move on; others are valued by several women, or many. The idea is not to discover "the truth" and, competitively, to present it more clearly or accurately or completely than anyone else; it is, rather, to contribute one's own words, insights, speculations, jokes, to feminist realities.

Indeed, in my experience, in writings that include accounts of an author's motives, questions of "truth" tend to give way to questions of honesty and authenticity. Because under the pressures of patriarchy it is a struggle for women to be honest and authentic with ourselves, I want to remember when I am writing to ask questions such as these: Do I contemplate these ideas in feminist consciousness, or as I have been taught in patriarchy to do? Do I think the succession of ideas myself or do I follow patriarchal patterns of words drummed into me? Am I trying to conform to certain ideals, for example, to prove that I made a choice in order to feel freer, when in fact I was forced? Am I giving false reasons for what I did choose in order to appear more acceptable to myself or to others? Am I failing to acknowledge the possibility of having forgotten what was too painful to remember? And so on.

Of course even if I am able to relate a story fully and without self-deception, there may be good reasons for not doing so. What if my mother reads this? My partner? My friends? The people I work with? My employer? Sometimes my concern about the reactions of others is exaggerated: what I was scared to say may, to my surprise, evoke little or no response, or be accepted with understanding and support. In other cases, though, there is danger in honesty: when women tell about ourselves, other people sometimes do withdraw their respect, their love, their money. In addition, when we tell about others in the process of telling about ourselves, we may, if the story is published, be subject to laws against invasion of privacy.

One way to avoid such consequences may be to tell one's stories as fiction: in fiction, one can work out parts of one's life on paper but then claim that it is "only a story." This approach may succeed, to some extent, in fooling others—or oneself: I may discover only later that what I have written about a character is, in some sense, true of me, or of someone close to me.

But I am concerned here with "feminist theory"—or, for plurality and process, "feminist theorizings"—not fiction. I am saying that I like theorizings to include accounts of what in the author's experience leads her to her topic and connects with her beliefs about it. There are not many models for such work: bell hooks' books show such connections, and so do the writings of Sonia Johnson; much of what is called feminist theory, however, follows the academic tradition of deliberately impersonal prose. (I myself tend to write in academic style; it is a method trained into me and hard to expel.) It is no accident, of course, that many beloved feminist theorists are not professional academics and so are not subject to the academy's tendency toward or insistence on anti-feminist methods.

My idea of "feminist theory," then, is that it consists of our stories, contradicting, overlapping, emotional, and hence not comprising a "machine." I believe that every woman, not just those who identify as theorists or writers, has stories of value to others.

But why call storytelling "theorizing"? A theory is supposed to be general or universal, it is supposed to propose or
claim something about many individuals, not just one. But this
concept of theory belongs to the kind of thought that has us
subordinated in the first place, to the kind of thought that
assigns to the writer the role of God. I want none of it.

But stories, even if "about" only one person, of course have
implications for others as well. A story that makes sense of
part of a woman's life includes accounts—"analyses"—of how
she is connected to people and practices and institutions
around her—and there are lots of general claims in that. So,
one might say, feminism develops a concept of theory as an
account of reality that does not move either inductively or
deductively between the general and particular but, rather,
sites the general in the particular. Someone trained in philosophy might say something like that.

I, however, would not. Indeed, I suspect that the idea of
theory repels or attracts on the basis of elitism: one woman
likes the idea of "doing theory" because it sounds important (I
include myself, at least an earlier self, here); another thinks
(usually correctly) that those who claim to do theory are trying
to show that they are better than some others. So I would prefer
to abandon the idea of theory/theorizings and to speak of
telling stories instead: Anyone can tell her story, stories may
be true and made up in various proportions, they can be mainly
about just one person, or about many, or about everyone, and
they tell more than they say. They include analyses and show
motives. They entertain, explain, connect, emancipate. Anyone
can take whatever she wants from them in the process of making her own stories/realities/selves, and we can together draw
on them in making cultures. For me it definitely makes more
sense to talk about stories than about theories or theorizings.

"ETHICS"

I find writing of the sort I have been discussing here so
valuable, so much preferable to academic treatments of ideas,

that—if I were to support the concept of "ethics" for lesbian and feminist work (it is too hierarchical for me)—I would be inclined to support an "ethics of method" that includes the idea that it is good when feminists and lesbians write about aspects of reality by telling stories, that is, by saying what they have to say in terms of their lives and the lives of women they care about. But I have decided not to try to persuade other women to adopt my values as their own, so I say here only that I do very much value such writing.

If many lesbian and feminist writers were to decide to adopt such a value, one advantage might be that some of the more boring women's studies work would never get written—for example, a scholar thinking about how her subject connects with her own daily life, or with her neighbor's or her sister's, might decide that it doesn't, and so shift her energies to a subject closer to her heart, which would surely make for livelier writing. Also, putting the writer in the work helps the reader to understand: if a sociologist writes about right-wing women, I want to know whether she does so because she herself is one, because she is merely curious, because she is a radical who writes out of the pain of having some women so distant from her, or for some other reason; knowing her motive helps me to make sense of what she says.

Sometimes lesbian and feminist writers explicitly identify themselves in terms of variables such as race, class, age, and region, in their works or in contributors' notes. I want this kind of information when I read but, as I suggest here, I also want more particular information. In a consciousness-raising group I belonged to in the early seventies that consisted of women philosophers (mostly graduate students), I remember discussing a text by a male philosopher and one of the women saying: "If this were written by a woman, she'd say what's bothering her."[1] I remember this remark because it captures for me a precious aspect of feminist and lesbian method. Lesbian and feminist authors often do say what is bothering us,

---

[1] Thanks to Karen Lucas.

which usually has to do with our particular thoughts, feelings, and experiences.

As for the present piece, I write it to "justify" the kind of work I like best to do. I like working best—at least in this part of my life—when I am making sense of my secrets. When I write out of memory and emotion, and make new connections among them, and connect them with concepts and values— then the work is most like what I have always wanted to do, and doing it feels good.

Back at that eastern college, it did not occur to me to discuss my own struggles with feelings as part of why I had chosen to write on the topic of emotion. It had not occurred to me because, in order to get the doctorate, I had to write in the voice of one who is simply trying to understand and improve the system of concepts about emotion, in the voice of a maintenance man. Now I try to be free from that constraint, so as to connect philosophizing with everyday life (such a simple idea) and, as I have said, I like it a lot when other writers do, too.

Thanks to Claudia Card for her help with this essay.

Not Lesbian Philosophy

Am I alone in being alone? I respond to a call for papers on lesbian philosophy because I believe that this rubric will connect me with women with ideas like mine. I respond even though, most deeply, I feel myself a lesbian only by default and hardly a philosopher at all.

Oh, I have a job as a philosopher, and if someone were to ask "How many lesbians in the room?" I'd raise my hand. But "philosopher" and "lesbian" aren't names I choose for myself. Currently, the name I like best is "anti-hierarchist"—that's an idea I can cling to. Among anti-hierarchists, I imagine, lesbians are dykes and no one has the role of philosopher, the role of an authority who tells other people how things are and should be and who, because of being a philosopher, is entitled to be believed.

A concept of a philosopher—white, male, oldish, "wise"—was transmitted to me as part of the culture in which I was conditioned, and then I learned more about it when I got to college and began taking philosophy courses in which the "superiority" of philosophy was taught along with Plato and symbolic logic. I loved much of what went on in those courses: the manipulation of symbols, the "certainty" of the analytic methods, the promise of being able to figure out what to believe and what to do with my life, the mystique of philosophy as difficult, profound, and of sublime importance. Philosophy was, after all, the "Queen of the Sciences"—what could be more suitable for a young woman who, when asked what she wanted to do with her life, would sometimes say that she intended to find out the "best" possible thing to do and then do it? The chairman of the philosophy department was of a different mind: he told me that philosophy was "not a good field for a girl"; but I insisted, and he relented. That philosophy admitted only a few women helped to maintain its status; that I was one of the few tended to elevate mine.

In graduate school, elitism training got serious. The message was both that philosophy is "superior" to other disciplines (whose problems ultimately lead one to philosophy) and that academics in general are "better" than most other people (only academics have a chance at understanding what's really going on, than which there is nothing more important, because understanding is the means for controlling nature, systems, and people—and no questioning the value of controlling). I was learning well. For example, when the teacher of a large introductory course I was required to attend as a teaching assistant began the semester by saying that although this was a course on philosophy he did not call himself a philosopher because whether he was a philosopher or not was for others to decide, I sneered; how silly, I thought—a transparent attempt to enhance his own status. I had already learned the importance of subtlety in inculcating the elitist message.

By the time I became an assistant professor, I was expected to be skilled in and thoroughly committed to the narrow path of analytic rigor, rejecting anything "soft," non-white, non-Anglo, non-supportive of the way my colleagues wanted to live. Further, if I wanted to "succeed," I would have to participate regularly in the dueling, the repartee, that they reveled in. But as the Second Wave of feminism broke, I had a framework for my resistance. I started to argue feminism with a powerful man on my tenure committee with whom I was having sex. He was not persuaded, I came out, got tenure, and gradually reduced my relationship with all my male colleagues to a distant cordiality.

If the philosophers who, over the years, tried to make me conform were to defend their own "superiority," their arguments might be versions (probably fancier and more obscure) of this one: A philosopher's function is to uncover TRUTHS that benefit "the whole society" (by trickle-down); these truths are not just lying around to be noticed by anyone but require special intelligence, training, and resources—a *discipline*—to be uncovered; hence, philosophers are and should be taken to be authorities on the subjects they discuss.

One difficulty here, in my mind, is that the "truths" philosophers discuss are mainly *values* that presuppose other, unstated values (for example, the superiority of white male methods or the inevitability of hierarchy). I can't consciously accept values that presuppose other values that I reject, and so the philosophers who propound them can't be "authoritative" for me. Perhaps it would help if thinkers would lay out all their presuppositions, but that's impossible because there is no end to presuppositions, no point at which the background of every idea has been completely explicated: each new expli- cation requires explication itself and, also, life won't hold still long enough—new stuff keeps happening. So, instead of knowing all of a thinker's assumptions, one has instead to con- sider that person's life and situation and make a guess about whether the deep values are likely to be similar to one's own. In order to make that comparison, of course, one must know quite a bit about one's own values. But if I know my own val- ues and also something about how to find out more about them, then I don't need an authority. Having developed a practice of discovering/creating my own values, I am my own "authority."

Another difficulty with the argument is in the claim that discovering "truths" requires a special discipline. In my expe- rience, it is part of the ordinary life of many dykes who have not had advanced training in an academic discipline to think seriously and critically about values. I understand that devel- oping a sustained presentation of ideas does require resources, particularly time and energy and concentration—but obvi- ously it doesn't require training and licensing, as in academe.

So I think that professional philosophers have no claim to authority over other people's beliefs both because in order to accept an authority one needs to be in the process of developing one's own values, which means that one doesn't need an authority, and because the training of professional philosophers gives no special capacity for finding "truth." In particular, I think that dykes who are professional philosophers have no claim to authority among dykes. Indeed, the fact that parts of the intellectual lives of many academic lesbians are directly influenced by dominant white males on a nearly daily basis is reason to be *especially* cautious about their/our contributions to dyke thought.

A main function of academic philosophy (and other academic disciplines) in the larger context of the dominant culture is to persuade people to accept hierarchies, for example by making power-over relationships appear natural, inevitable, or good or, more subtly, by promising power-over (sometimes by implying that if you can understand *this* obscure/complex/boring stuff, you're "better" than other people). By rationalizing hierarchy, philosophers strengthen the power of those hierarchically above them, secure their own places in the structure, and ensure that large numbers remain below. Maverick academics who don't want to play this game either do not survive—we get kicked out or down (many political dykes once in academe have left and many are part-time, peripheral); or we are tolerated as tokens; or we do a lot of pretending, hiding our true values, our true selves, from our colleagues and perhaps from ourselves; or we compromise by changing our true values/selves.

In any case, it seems clear to me—and, I expect, to most of the readers of this essay—that academic philosophy, "analytic" and otherwise, as it exists today in the u.s. and at least some other places, is essentially oppressive, in part because most of its practitioners, following tradition, assume that they have a right to determine how other people should think and act. Why would a dyke want to be associated with such an enterprise?

Money, of course. I and others maintain a relationship with a philosophy department primarily so that we can buy what we need and/or so we can control our own money. Once, when I was just about to enter a ph.d. program, a faculty member asked me why I had decided to come back to school and I told him that I needed the money (I thought then that I could speak honestly to faculty); I remember his disdain as he said that scholarly work should be done only by those who would do it for love even if no money were involved. But I knew that if I didn't need money, I would be moving around the world writing and reading and exploring, as I had been doing before—not going to school. This middle-aged, white, upper-middle-class male, who felt quite at home in the university, taught me something about academe and about himself by his remark. He learned nothing from me, though; he had no idea how being in school felt to me.

But philosophy for me is not just a matter of money. Sometimes I use my connection with philosophy as a source of status. I do so for good purpose when, for example, I use being a professor at the university to get access to resources for lesbian and feminist groups. But I also identify with the status sometimes when I have no such purpose because, like most people conditioned in hierarchical society (like all, I believe, who have not consciously changed), I have a hierarchical grid within me that puts people into slots according to what I imagine to be their value compared to me, usually either above or below. Although I work on dissolving this grid, it still operates within me much of the time.

Philosophy gives me a sounder sort of self-esteem too: I am proud that I was able to survive mid-century u.s. society by learning how to get paid by a university. Without being able to write and teach and have *some* control over my work, I would have had a much worse time.

But apart from my reasons for maintaining an association with institutionalized philosophy, I like some of the kinds of thinking and talking that go under the name "philosophy." These, of course, don't require academe. Indeed, it can be argued that "dyke philosophy" can barely be done—or at least can't thrive—in academe. In any case, for me, calling the antihierarchizing exploration of ideas "philosophy" brings hierarchy back in; for me, the terms "philosophy" and "philosopher" seem irredeemably contaminated with elitism.

But "dyke" has been redefined, why not "philosophy"? I don't mean here to suggest attempting to reform philosophy within academe. Much feminist work in academe, including the development of women's studies, helps make it a better place for women, but I think that the university will continue to be dedicated to hierarchizing people and that reform efforts need to be infused with that awareness. Outside of academe, however, "philosophy" is used to refer to a certain subject matter, a certain approach to thinking, that can and perhaps in some cultures does exist not only without reference to academe but perhaps also without assuming authority over knowledge. Perhaps "philosophy" can be and sometimes is used in such a way among dykes. Western academics do not own philosophy, although many think that they do.

Even now, in some dyke communities, dykes have a sense of "philosophy" whereby the term refers not to a professional role but to a kind of talk, or talk-action, that occurs alongside other forms such as telling about the past, making plans, explaining how to do something. It would be interesting to know whether, in such groups, philosophizing is a function supposed to be performed by only a few or is taken to be something nearly everyone does or can do. I am inclined to prefer the latter arrangement because I so much want each dyke's ideas and feelings to be valued, to be valued "equally." That many dykes are committed to processes whereby *every* womon is given serious attention and respect is, for me, part of the genius of dykes together, one of the great joys of being a dyke.

But the likelihood of the term "philosophy" being reconceived and becoming a regular part of the vocabulary of wimmin's spaces is small, I think, at least where there is proximity to academe. It is one thing to wipe the dirt off "dyke," but quite another to wipe the power-over off "philosopher."

So although I have a job as a philosopher, "philosopher" is not a name I choose for myself. Nor do I now have—or need—a substitute.

"Philosopher" is not a name I choose, and neither is "lesbian." Regarding "lesbian" I will be brief. Although I like the company in this category a lot better than that in the category "philosopher," I reject its focus. In my experience, the meaning of "lesbian" is primarily sexual. Lesbian literature includes discussions intended to shift the meaning of lesbianism away from sex to other centers such as friendship or the rejection of patriarchy, but many, perhaps most, lesbians nevertheless define "lesbian" as centrally about sex, as do most heterosexuals.

But I am not primarily sexual and so do not like being named with a word that means "sex" to most people; defining women in terms of sex is a trick men play on women and I don't want to play it on myself. Sexuality is in me, in my life. It has had a VERY IMPORTANT role in my development, as is virtually inevitable in patriarchy. But I think of sexuality—sexuality/violence—as the main tool that men and boys use to control women and girls. Like some other lesbians, I certainly do not want it as a central part of my identity.

Instead of "lesbian," I prefer "dyke," with its message of resistance: "dyke" speaks more to—and of—my heart.

But why do I want to reject the name "lesbian philosopher"? I have just given reasons, but why are these reasons salient for me, why do I make them mine? Reasons are based on motives, in my opinion: one is moved by feelings rooted in one's situation, experiences, and temperament to find and adopt particular values along with reasons for them. So I want here to touch upon some of the parts of my background that are relevant to my dislike of "lesbian philosopher."

First, the process of detaching myself from academic philosophy occurs at this particular time in my life because, at fifty-nine, I begin to see the end of my economic reliance on the university. In a half dozen years or less I will "retire" and, while some think of retirement as extended leave and continue with their academic identities, to me it is an opportunity for restructuring my work and, to some extent, myself. Having resigned from the university, I intend to be something less polite than a lesbian philosopher. At school the politeness is a protection from men in my immediate environment, but when I leave my job, there will rarely be men in my immediate environment. At that time I would like to be able to be simply a dyke, a dyke whose life includes writing and thinking about ideas—although I know that I will not shed my academic identity easily, quickly, or all at once.

My preparation for rejecting hierarchy, including both academe and heterosexuality, began in infancy. According to my mother, during my first few weeks of life I was often left alone in a room where I screamed from frustration and loneliness, wanting to be held, wanting company, feeling abandoned. The doctor had warned my mother that if she followed her feelings and picked me up whenever I cried between feedings, she would "spoil" me. So, trying to be a good mother, she left me alone. I screamed, enraged. I take this experience to be a first and deep lesson in the importance for me of being in control of my own situation.

My mother and I continued to have battles of will. I remember, for example, that when I was four or five she made me sit all afternoon over my lunch—strained spinach with bits of bacon in it, long gone cold—insisting that I eat; I refused. I was testing my power, learning the range of an idea that was to become part of the long-term music of my mind: "You can't make me." For many years, this refrain, "You can't make me," played over and over in my head along with another favorite, "My mother won't let me": songs of a dominated child. My mother's intention, which was supported by my father, was that every aspect of my life—behavior and appearance, thoughts and feelings—should be as she wanted (of course she read my locked diary: I remember putting a hair on a page to test her, and the next day it was gone). Being thus dominated prepared me to resist hierarchy both by making me super-aware of the frustration of not being in control of one's own life and by giving me practice in feeling alone, in being an outsider with respect to those who did not question hierarchy.

As I grew older, I struggled to reject my family of origin and also decided that I would not myself marry or give birth; later, I rejected the very concept of family, and now I want not to use that term at all, not even for dykes relating to dykes, because for me it inevitably resonates hierarchy—not only the hierarchy of my own particular experiences, but, more generally, the domination of females, of the young, and of the old that is part of the meaning of "family" in mainstream culture. In my teens and twenties I rejected also conventional ideas about work. I had no patience for any of the "careers" that I was supposed to choose from and devoted my energies instead to ideas, art, and adventure, partly for love of intense experience and partly because I needed such experiences, I thought, in order to know how to live. I was called a nonconformist, a "bohemian," and, in my mother's word, a "drifter." (I remember being thrilled with the label "nonconformist"—a name for myself! It was perhaps as welcome to me then as "lesbian" has been to dykes-from-birth who grew up without any reflection of themselves.)

So, one might say, I rejected conventional values because of the combination of my temperament and my mother's domination of me and I was able to choose to be unconventional partly because I had learned to be by myself, growing up in a household where I was alone in confronting the monolithic power of my parents, and by myself also in the wider social context where my values were unacceptable to most of the people around me. With this background, I was of course overwhelmed when I finally learned, with the advent of feminism, that there are *good reasons* for my differences, that is, that my hatred of being controlled, my rejection of family, my refusal to conform to other people's standards, that all this resistance makes intellectual sense in the context of analyses of the

oppression of women and children, of capitalism, of heterosexism, of hierarchy.

As I continue to discover/invent "theory" to attach to my
deepest feelings and as I become more connected with other
dykes, I realize also that I am *not* alone, not, at any rate,
entirely alone. While no one else rejects the names "lesbian"
and "philosopher" for just the same reasons I do (no one else
has just the same stories), I am not alone in the rejecting. Anti-
hierarchist dykes—disagreeing with one another on all manner
of topics including what constitutes anti-hierarchism—abound.

*Ideas from Chris Cuomo and Sally Tatnall have been helpful for this writing (I
heard both of them speak about philosophy at a meeting of the Society for Women
in Philosophy in Edwardsville, Illinois, on March 7, 1992).*

*I appreciate also responses to an earlier version of the piece—but the rewrit-
ing has changed it so much that the earlier "version" is really a different piece—
by Claudia Card, Marilyn Friedman, and two anonymous reviewers.*

COMPETITION

Competition

Competition among species, to explain evolution. Competition among ideas, as a way of finding truth. Competition for profits. For power. To be number one.

Competition for attention, grades, love, sex, jobs, money, fame, to be best. About how smart you are. About how attractive you are.

Feeling superior.

Feeling inferior.

Ordinary life in patriarchy.

At one of the early conferences of the National Women's Studies Association, the organization's first award was announced—a writing prize, I think—and I was dismayed to realize that no one seemed even to notice what I took to be a selling-out of feminism: the deliberate creation of unnecessary competition among women. Within a few years, the association was sponsoring a variety of prizes and scholarships without, as far as I know, ever providing a forum about whether these competitions fit with feminist values. Perhaps I should not have been surprised. But having had strong hopes that the association would be a place where I could be comfortable, I felt betrayed.

More recently, Valerie Miner and Helen E. Longino edited a feminist anthology about competition.[1] In it they call for the

---

[1] *Competition: A Feminist Taboo?* edited by Valerie Miner and Helen E. Longino (New York: The Feminist Press, 1987).

development of "appropriate" and "healthy" competition in
the context of communities committed to "mutual assistance,
reciprocity, and the general welfare" (178). Reading this, I
again felt distressed and disappointed. Is competing "appropriate" and "healthy" for the wimmin who lose?

The main difference between me and feminists who support competition, I think, is that they tend to focus on winners
and on those who are challenged and inspired by competing;
but I think mainly of losers.

I don't formally compete much anymore, but I used to,
especially in school. Now I compete mainly in less explicit, less
conscious ways—in social situations, in meetings, sometimes in
writing. I compete because I want the attention that goes to
winners, attention that helps me feel that I'm okay. I compete to
test myself, to find out *whether* I'm acceptable or not, much as a
gambler does. I compete still, sometimes because I want confir-
mation of my opinion that I'm not worth shit.

I remember responding to losing with "but I followed all
the rules, I did everything you're supposed to do, I gave up
everything else," which is a way of saying that I *really* am no
good and there's nothing I can do about it (with a glimmer of
satisfaction). I remember envy so intense I have withdrawn
entirely. I remember winning and thinking, "I don't want the
prize unless the others have one too."

I assume that I am not alone among wimmin in responding
to competition in these ways. So I want to be rid of competition; I am unwilling to support a system that fosters such feelings. Some critics would say that the problem is not in the system but in the psyches. I say that competition creates and then
exercises elements in (some) dyke psyches that, if left unstim-
ulated, would very likely wither away.

The short form of what I have to say here is this: Competition by definition creates losers. Because I don't want to be a
party to turning wimmin into losers, I don't want competitions in the dyke spaces I participate in.

(On the definition of competition: The purpose of competition as such is to rank participants, to distinguish "better" from "worse," "superior" from "inferior." An activity in which everyone "wins" or from which everyone benefits equally is not a competition.)

(On turning wimmin into losers: I assume that when a woman enters a competition voluntarily she wants to win [and perhaps also not to win]. A competitor who doesn't win has her desire to win frustrated [one who does win—a much rarer case—may also be frustrated]. I don't want to support practices that frustrate wimmin.)

In the u.s. and elsewhere, sport is set up as the model for all competition. In sport, the rules are assumed to be known to all the players; referees or umpires are supposed to ensure fairness; and often, I gather, it really is true that the individual or team who plays hardest and most skillfully wins. This model encourages people to believe that life is like a footrace or a baseball game: how well-off one is depends on how successfully one competes. Happiness is supposed to come from the prizes one wins through competing successfully (fame, money, relative freedom) and, of course, even more from having a sense of oneself as a winner—from feeling oneself superior to others.

In fact, however, except for a few celebrities who are made into icons at least partly to promote competition, in capitalist hierarchy goods are distributed almost entirely according to familiar rankings such as race, class, gender, age, sexual orientation, ability, and so on, with large numbers of people getting a disproportionately small share of goods. Most of these hierarchies are, and I believe those at the pinnacles intend them to be, fixed and inherited. Boys who are born white and rich are intended to keep their privileges throughout their lives without ever having to compete for them, and to pass their positions on to their "legitimate" sons; except for the tokens who prove the rule, no one else can hold those positions no matter what they achieve in competition. Similarly, women of all races and classes, no matter how "well" we "perform," are intended to be permanently excluded from serious power. Children are everywhere denied self-determination, and are expected to treat their own children the same when they grow up. And so on.[2]

Within the major ranks of race, age, etc., competition is used to assign people to specific positions. Employees compete for jobs; friends and associates compete to be, for example, "smartest" or "wildest" or "most successful." Some such situations may really function on the game model, rewarding the most "deserving," and so providing evidence for the belief that living well is a function of competitive success. But in these competitions, very little is at stake. Differences between people with respect to sex, class, race, and the like are far greater than those that are determined on the basis of competition. The differences between the opportunities available to the valedictorian of an upper-class preparatory school and the valedictorian of a working-class public high school, for example, are for the most part larger than those between the opportunities available to the valedictorian of either school and other students at that school, except where factors such as sex or race add another dimension of difference. While people are busy competing, the outlines of their futures are already settled on the basis of who they are, their inheritance. I don't mean that the small increments that can be won or lost through competition are worthless, only that they make relatively tiny differences within inherited ranks.

Competition works within hierarchy for the assignment of places within the categories of oppression and also, occasion-

---

[2]Statuses that are not inherited include acquired disability and lesbianism that is at least partly chosen. Acquired disability fits the pattern of the inherited statuses in that an individual with such a disability is not responsible for it (self-inflicted physical disability is attributed to unchosen psychological disability). Chosen lesbianism, however, is a problem for this ideology. It is a problem for gay men who base arguments for their inclusion in the mainstream on the idea that "homosexuality" is innate, and it is also a problem for heterosexists whose sense of superiority is based partly on the notion that they were born superior.

ally, in connection with really moving from one category to another. For example, a woman, if she is enough like a man while still being enough like a woman, may win token power in a powerful organization. Or an individual may move to a "lower" category on the basis of failing in competition—or, perhaps more commonly, by refusing to play at all. But mainly, in my observation, you get what your inheritance warrants. And that can't be changed by an individual.

A main function of competition, then, in dominant "western" societies, is as a mask for the hierarchies it helps sustain. Competition is necessary for systems of domination to work. The oppressed won't submit if they/we don't believe that the oppressors "really are" superior, and giving dominators prizes (e.g., riches, rights, knowledge, guns) establishes the "fact" of their superiority .

So people are trained to believe that competitions for jobs and educations and money and power are like sports, where upstarts and underdogs can win through skill, practice, and dedication, but in reality the rewards and penalties determined by competitions are almost always trivial and the hierarchies are as fixed as (but ultimately no more permanent than) those in a medieval fiefdom.

Having given some indication of the context of my own dislike of competition, it's time to attend to some reasons wimmin give for liking it.

Self-esteem:

"Competition fosters excellence."[3]
"Competition inspires me to do my best."

---

[3] For an important distinction between two senses of excellence, which shows that one can do excellent work in a context that doesn't involve comparison, consult "Competition, Compassion, and Community: Models for a Feminist Ethos" by María C. Lugones and Elizabeth V. Spelman in *Competition: A Feminist Taboo* edited by Valerie Miner and Helen E. Longino (New York: The Feminist Press, 1987), 234-47.

"Competition teaches self-confidence."
"Competition gives me incentive to develop my skills."
"Competition answers my curiosity about what I can do."
"Competition focuses the mind."
"Competition is a source of discipline."
"Competition elicits courage."
"Competition makes me tough."

Thrills:

"Competition is exciting."
"Competition is challenging."
"Competition makes me feel alive."
"Competition turns me on."

I have been talking with feminists and lesbians about competition on and off for years, and the reasons in favor of competition that I mention here come either from these conversations or from feminist writings or both. I believe them all. That is, I believe that competition really does sometimes have the effects claimed and that some wimmin value them. I am not, of course, concerned to "refute" any of these claims.

I do want to say that I don't *like* basing self-esteem, for example, on competing. For how does this work? The self-esteem, if it requires competing, must come from feeling oneself superior to others. Of course one could simply do the thing in question and be pleased with one's performance—run a marathon, say, and take pride in finishing—but in this case feeling good comes from completing the distance or completing it in a certain time, not from competing. (Competing against one's own previous best performance is a peculiar case because there is no person one is competing with; the previous self no longer exists. I am inclined to say that this is not competition at all.)

Obviously, competing is not the only means to self-esteem or thrills. I can feel respect for myself because I do a useful/beautiful/interesting/funny/whatever piece of work, where the value of the work is not based on any comparison. I can feel thrilled, sexy (the connection between competition and sexiness connects to the tie between competition and power/violence and so to the heart of the trouble with male-driven worlds)—I can feel thrilled by dykes celebrating together, by a long view of the desert, by a surprise, all without competition. So, rather than participate in making losers through competition, I want other sources of self-esteem and thrills.

In terms of practical politics, in some spaces I want to work on eliminating competition, while in others I root for dykes who are competing or I compete myself. How I actually respond to the fact of competition depends in part on the kind of space in which it takes place.

In what I call wimmin's spaces, or dyke spaces, dykes are developing anti-hierarchical values by resisting hierarchies and making ways to live without them and are healing self-hate by giving each womon enough attention. Wimmin's space is momentary or ongoing, everywhere around or hidden in the interstices of patriarchy. It is made by just one dyke in and around her self alone or by dykes in interaction with one another. In dyke spaces there often is hierarchy and competitiveness, but my idea is that a fundamental value shared by many of the wimmin interacting in such space is to change that.

"Dyke space" also means ideal or utopian dyke space, spaces where dykes already have lived through and past the struggle against hierarchy and competition. I am interested in ideal dyke space because I need to know how I want to live. But I try to resist my tendency to let this focus distract me from what is real, from the actual dyke spaces that are intermixed with patriarchy; from the processes of transition; and from learning more about what other dykes want, which changes my ideal.

Hierarchical or patriarchal space is, roughly speaking, all the rest. Most dykes do—must—spend time in competitive patriarchal situations for at least parts of our lives, typically in school and at work. My idea is not necessarily to resist competing in these settings; sometimes there is good reason to participate. When a dyke competes in patriarchy, I usually root for her.

(For a while I thought of the practice of resisting hierarchical society as a third kind of space, a sort of straddling between dyke space and patriarchy. Now I think that when I take my stand as a dyke and confront those in power, refusing to do what they want, I may be within dyke space; paying attention to what is outside is not necessarily to BE outside. In any case, resisting is not competing, but refusing to compete.)

So in dyke space, I want there not to be competition and competitiveness because I can't stand losing and I hate for other wimmin to lose, and because competition and competitiveness tend to both cover-up and sustain hierarchy, making it harder to detect and destroy.

But the short version of my dislike of competition is this: competition necessarily creates losers.

Envy

One of my friends is a writer.

I support her in her work and I admire what she writes.

Underneath I think: Her work is really not very good.

This is a wish, not a "literary judgment" (except insofar as all literary judgments are wishes).

Why don't I want this friend's work to be good?

  —Because it's very different from mine, so if hers is good, mine's not.

  (Objection: There is NOT only one kind of good work.)

Why don't I want her work to be good?

  —Because I work at writing many more hours than she does and if her work is as good as mine, then what's the point of all my hours and rewritings?

(Objection: It's a mistake to expect proportionality between effort and quality of product in any field.)

Why don't I want her writing to be good?

—Because I want only mine to be good.

(Objection: But this is absurd.)

TO ESCAPE THIS ABSURDITY:

Imagine a world in which each person is good at one thing and no one else is good at that thing.

—But real worlds of wimmin are/can be like that: Every womon does something or other in her own way and no one else does that thing in that way, so only she is "good" at what she does. But then the concept of good drops out because what a womon does is appreciated for itself and as expressive of who she is and is not; it does not need to be compared with what others do.

It's the systems of judgments that are corrupt; the creativity of wimmin is just fine.

Each womon is *the* expert on what she does.

EACH WOMON'S WORK IS UNIQUE AND SO IS THE "BEST" OF ITS KIND.

II

But that doesn't help much.

I realize that I'm not envious of my friend's work after all, but of her *success*, of the attention, admiration, and appreciation she gets that tell her that her work is worthwhile and so that she is okay. It's her *success* that prompts me to judge her work as "really not very good."

Why don't I want my friend to be successful?

—Because I believe that success is scarce. If she uses up some of the store, less is available for me.

(No objection. This is true. The amount of success possible in a community is limited by the time and energy people have to attend to one another's productions. All dykes together do not have time and energy enough to make every one among them/us successful.)

(Objection: But success needn't be scarce in a *small* group. Among just a few wimmin, each one can receive enough attention for even a soaring self-esteem.)

(Objection to the objection: A small group doesn't count.)

Why doesn't a small group count?

—Because of the meaning of "success." I am successful only if many people, including strangers, find my work worthwhile. And I am okay only if I am successful.

(Objection: But this is absurd.)

I DON'T KNOW HOW TO DEAL WITH THIS ABSURDITY.

III

I'm okay only if I can con a lot of people into paying attention
to me.

> It's a con because I know that no matter what I do, I am no
> more deserving of attention, success, FAME, than any-
> one else.

> No one is more deserving than anyone else.

> Being deserving has nothing do to with it.

Exactly.

It has to be a lot of people who pay attention to me because
the system is set up so that privileged and ambitious people have to devote immense effort to diluted work, work
that appeals across differences, in order to achieve success.

> But why?

>> —So that privileged, ambitious, creative people are mean-
>> inglessly, apolitically, occupied.

But that's not dykes.

No, of course not.

IV

But that doesn't help much.

I realize that I'm not envious of my friend's success after all,
but of her ability to receive, to revel in, attention.

How she loves to be the star! How she is always making it
happen that she *is* the star!

But if *I* am asked to be at the center, I decline: such events tire
me, I say—travel, strangers, always being "on." I would
rather be alone—

(Is there something else?

Do I *need* to feel deprived?

Deprived of attention, as I was as an infant, abandoned for
hours at a time?)

I NEED TO FEEL I NEED ATTENTION.

Maybe.

V

That doesn't help at all.

I play a trick on my psyche. I get myself believing that I can
have lots more attention than I in fact get, that I can have
enough.

Then I will tend to envy less.

—Because I will believe that I deserve attention as much as she does, as is proven by the fact that if I wanted attention I could get it.

Then I will feel distant from her and from the audience out there, and just go on in my own way, as I like to do, without comparing myself to her or to anyone—I'm not even a player anymore after all, I'm just working on my work—

It's ABSURD to trick myself.

VI

I will discipline my mind to stop thinking about her and other writers and their books.

—As I wrote that line, the phone rang with an invitation to a book-signing, an old friend is coming into town to promote her new novel—

I must empty my mind of what hurts me—

VII

I must get clear about what's going on: Sometimes lesbians give me attention and I enjoy it. At other times, though, I reject attention, because I like the feeling of needing it.

When I reject attention, I also want it, so I am in conflict.

The part of the conflict wherein I *want* attention feels like envy.

The part of the conflict wherein I do *not* want attention feels like home.

SEX

Taking Responsibility
for Sexuality

This essay, which was written before any of the others in this volume, was part of an ongoing discussion in midwestern SWIP (Society for Women in Philosophy) about the politics of sexuality. For a number of years—in the seventies and early eighties—lesbians had been presenting papers to the group about lesbianism, especially about connections between lesbianism and feminism. Nonlesbians sometimes contributed to discussions of lesbianism but most had little or nothing to say about their own sexual orientation and its relationships to feminism.

Some of the lesbians, including me, wanted the heterosexuals to become more deeply engaged in the philosophy of sex. I liked some of these women and wanted to know them better and to find out what they thought about sex; I also hoped for some comings-out. I thought that the process of taking responsibility for one's own sexual identity, which I urge here, would mean that I would have more lesbian friends.

I was writing especially for—or to—a particular woman, a heterosexual friend in SWIP with whom I had been having long discussions about a wide range of feminist ideas. We would see each other at SWIP meetings (held each semester at a different campus in the midwest) and sit up late at night after the evening sessions in her or my hotel room, usually with a bottle of wine, to talk about what was going on at the

*meetings and about our own work in feminist philosophy. I
was not hoping for a sexual relationship with her—that part
of my life was quite full enough already—but I liked her very
much and wished that we could share the lesbian values that
colored all of my ideas. I could not understand, then, why she
was not a lesbian. She read the essay. She discussed it with
me. She did not come out.*

*I was disappointed, but my disappointment was tem-
pered as time went on and I learned that other women who
read the essay, particularly young women in women's studies classes, were using it as part of their coming-out processes.*

It is fundamental to feminism that women should take responsibility for ourselves collectively and individually. In this essay
I explore a central aspect of this project: taking responsibility
for sexuality. I am particularly concerned here with women's
taking responsibility for our sexual identities as lesbian or heterosexual.

I write in part out of the struggle within feminism over
whether feminism precludes women's having affectional-sex-
ual ties with men. As those familiar with feminist theory know,
feminists advocate lesbianism on a variety of grounds. Some
emphasize, for instance, that because virtually everyone's first
erotic relationship is with a woman (mother), lesbianism is
"natural" for women, as heterosexuality is for men. Another
approach is based on the claim that in patriarchy, equality in a
heterosexual relationship is impossible; even if a man under-
takes to renounce male privileges, he cannot do so entirely. A
third argument holds that women committed to feminism
should give all their energies to women. I am not concerned
here to explore these positions. Rather, I want to develop the
idea of women's taking responsibility for our own sexuality,
whatever it may be. Feminism requires at least this of us.

Notice first that to take responsibility for a state of affairs is
not to claim responsibility for having caused it. So, for exam-

ple, if I take responsibility for cleaning up the kitchen I am not thereby admitting to any role in creating the mess; the state of the kitchen may be the consequence of actions quite independent of me. Similarly, in taking responsibility for sexual orientation, a woman is not thereby claiming responsibility for what her sexuality has been, but only for what it is now and in the future.[1]

To take responsibility for one's sexuality, or sexual identity, is to take responsibility for who one is not only in explicitly sexual relationships but as a whole person. Sexuality affects how one experiences and understands oneself and one's place in the world; whether one gives primary attention to women or men or both; how one spends energies; what one wants and wishes; the appearance one presents; and often also the work one does, where one lives, where one travels, more. To take responsibility for sexuality is to take responsibility for an aspect of oneself that pervades every part of personality.

In this writing, when I speak of taking responsibility for sexuality I am thinking primarily of taking responsibility for oneself as lesbian or heterosexual or bisexual, or as a celibate version of one of these, particularly as a feminist may define these terms for herself. I do not directly address other sexual identities, such as pansexual or omnisexual, sadomasochistic, "self-sexual," or radically celibate. Some women refuse to accept any label; I think that this position can also be a case of

---

[1] In feminist discourse, the concept of responsibility is sometimes avoided because it suggests rigid, hierarchical judgments. The notion of accountability is sometimes used instead. While being accountable is similar to taking responsibility in that one chooses what one is accountable for (one is not accountable if one did not make the commitment), it differs in that it emphasizes relationships. Accountability calls attention to those to whom one is accountable—one's group, friends, lover; to urge that women should accept accountability for their sexuality is to urge them to accept membership in a group or, anyway, to make a commitment to some relationship. In this essay, I use responsibility instead of accountability because my focus is not so much on a woman's relationship to other women as on her giving reasons, perhaps only to herself, for her sexual practices.

taking responsibility for one's own sexual identity. In any case, I do not mean here to claim that feminists "should" take responsibility for sexuality, but only to explore some of what is involved for those who choose to do so.

A paradigm case of taking responsibility for one's sexuality is coming out as a lesbian. It is characteristic of first coming out, of coming out to oneself, that a woman does not know whether to say that she has *discovered* that she is a lesbian, or that she has *decided* to be a lesbian. The experience is one of acknowledging, of realizing what is already there, and at the same time of creating something new, a new sense of oneself, a new identity. In coming out, one connects an already-existing reality—sensations, feelings, identification with women—with a new understanding or concept of who one is. This is the sort of process I mean to refer to here when I speak of taking responsibility for sexuality.[2]

The process, then, is one of *discovery/creation*. Notice that there is no brief expression in ordinary English that captures this concept. It might be suggested that coming out is a matter of "interpretation," of interpreting or reinterpreting one's experiences and feelings in a certain way, as evidence of or elements in one's lesbianism. But this way of understanding coming out is incomplete because it captures only part of the process, the discovery part. To discover that one has been a lesbian all along is to interpret past experiences in a new way, as experiences of a closeted lesbian. But coming out involves also deciding to be a lesbian, which is to say deciding not to participate in the institution of heterosexuality and to (continue to) love women. Coming out is not merely a matter of reinterpreting one's past; it involves taking responsibility for being a lesbian both in the past and in the future.

Another received idea that might be thought to apply to coming out is that of a conversion experience. There is cer-

---

[2] For coming-out stories consult, for example, *The Original Coming Out Stories*, second edition, edited by Julia Penelope and Susan J. Wolfe (Freedom, Calif.: The Crossing Press, 1989).

tainly ample patriarchal literature about people undergoing conversions, mostly religious. But the idea of conversion doesn't capture coming out either. The patriarchal convert becomes what he was not. The lesbian becomes what she is.

But, it might be suggested, what about the expression "coming out" itself? Doesn't that convey the experience? This expression has been adopted by lesbians from gay male culture and by gay males presumably from the custom of debutantes coming out into society. It emphasizes not the creation of the self, but the presentation of the self to others. It omits, I think, the inwardness of lesbian experience, the fact that coming out is not merely (or at all) a social process but a subjective one, a kind of growth.

It is no accident, of course, that there is no term in patriarchy for the experience I am concerned with here, that there is no brief way of accurately referring to it. Patriarchy, although it takes different forms in different cultures, always depends on the ability of men to control women through heterosexuality: the idea of the father, the patriarch, is the idea of a male who controls the sexual activity of the mother—else how would he know that he was the father?—and the idea of male domination (a meaning of "patriarchy" that does not focus on fatherhood) is centrally the idea of males having sexual access to females as the males want, not according to the wills of the females (who aren't even supposed to have wills). Were large numbers of women to take responsibility for our own sexuality and in so doing reject heterosexuality, the very concepts of woman and man would be shattered. Thus, men, committed to the preservation of patriarchy for the sake of their own power-over and identities, make a language with no words for women's resistance, with no words for women taking responsibility for our own sexual identities.[3]

---

[3] In patriarchy, women may be expected to take responsibility for certain aspects of their sexuality, for example, for allowing sexual access only to males of their own race or for birth control. But the idea that a woman can take responsibility for her sexual orientation, for herself as lesbian or heterosexual, is foreign to patriarchy.

Before I go on to discuss the meaning of taking responsibility for sexual orientation for heterosexual women, I want to indicate briefly some of the ways patriarchy insists that sexuality is wholly given. Because patriarchs cannot allow most women to choose against heterosexuality, the preferred patriarchal position is that heterosexuality is a *given*, something about oneself that one cannot change. Patriarchs want women to believe that we are fundamentally heterosexual and that we can neither alter our dispositions to be sexual only with men nor reject sexuality entirely, so we must make do as heterosexual, however distasteful that may be. But if sexuality is a given, why is it that some people are not heterosexual?

That sexuality is a *given* is generally taken to mean that it is based in biology (which many believe is itself ordained by deity). In this context, if a woman is sexually interested in other women, either something is wrong with her body—perhaps she has a "hormonal imbalance," for example—or she suffers from psychological or spiritual difficulties that prevent her from following her "natural" inclinations.

If sexuality is biological, the question of taking responsibility for one's orientation does not arise for either lesbians or heterosexuals. Sexuality for everyone is something one "gets," something that happens to one, and if it is not okay, then an expert may be called in—physician, psychiatrist, priest—but the woman herself remains passive, submissive, with respect to her sexual identity.

But the idea that sexuality is biological is used not only as part of the apparatus of enforced heterosexuality; it is also the basis for an argument for assimilation used by some gay males and lesbians. Instead of holding that biology always aims to produce heterosexuals, they claim that biology creates different sexual orientations—heterosexual in some people and gay or lesbian in others. Hence, they continue, discrimination against gays and lesbians is unjust because one cannot help one's biology or, therefore, one's sexuality. In terms of respecting the freedom of women to discover/create our own sexuality, this position is no improvement over the more traditional, monolithic idea that only heterosexuality is biologically given; both positions define women as subject to our biology and fail to acknowledge our right to take responsibility for and name our own sexualities.

Yet another version of the analysis of sexuality as biological holds that everyone is innately "pansexual" or, at least, bisexual. The point of this claim is usually to argue that "everyone," which in practice often means women rather than men, should be open to whatever sorts of sexual encounters those making the claim, who have generally been men, want them to engage in. Here again a theoretical idea about biology is used as a way of controlling women's sexuality.

A different account of the origin of sexuality as a given attributes it not to biology but mainly to one's experiences in early childhood. This position usually appears in the context of a traditional value system according to which "normal" experience produces only heterosexuality and everything else is a disease or deviation. In any case, the structure of the early experience explanation is the same as the structure of biological explanations. Sexuality is a given, and women's role with respect to it therefore must be passive; what a woman is, sexually, is determined by something that happened to her and that she herself cannot change.

None of these male-created systems allows space for the idea that one might discover/create one's own sexuality on the basis of one's feelings and one's politics, on the basis of reasons, on the basis of the rational-emotional weighing of all those factors one deems relevant. Patriarchal accounts of the origins of sexuality leave no space for women to participate in the discovery/creation of our own sexual identities. A feminist theory of sexuality that would suit me would not be a causal theory in any familiar sense, and it would surely include an account of the role a woman herself may play in the development of her sexuality. Also, in my feminism, identity is not based on what one does with one's genitals or on whether one has certain sorts of sensations or feelings, but on enacted values. What are a woman's values, how does she live? What are her politics? Answers to these questions, which I believe need to include information about a woman's relationships with others, tell me what I want to know about who women are. In this essay, however, my interest in identity has a narrower focus: I discuss sexual identity as having to do primarily with genital activity because this patriarchal concept is, in my experience, usually taken for granted by women who do *not* take responsibility for their sexuality. Men, of course, tend to profit from women's thinking of heterosexuality and lesbianism in narrowly physical and emotional terms rather than as ways of addressing power.

"Coming out," as I have suggested, provides a model for the process of taking responsibility for sexual orientation. But what could it possibly mean to "come out" as a heterosexual? Most heterosexual women accept the identities their conditioning provides for them and so, it would seem, there is little or nothing for them to discover or create.

But to think in this way is again to fall into the trap of taking sexuality as merely given. Virtually all women can take responsibility for our own sexuality. For a heterosexual woman to take responsibility for herself as heterosexual involves her acknowledging the elements of her life that count as heterosexual and, also, making decisions about whether, when, and how to participate in heterosexuality. Notice that heterosexuality is an institution with many facets. It consists not just of sexual activity, but of a myriad of values and practices, including, for example, concepts of love, of couples, of faithfulness; meanings given to various styles in clothes and personal appearance; ways of behaving with men and with women; and so on. A heterosexual woman taking responsibility decides which of the aspects of the institution she wishes to participate in (if any), and why. She may participate wholly, but if she is responsible, she does so not without thinking but, generally, for reasons that she takes to be good ones.

Some women object to the idea of taking responsibility for their own sexual identity on the ground that they are what they are—lesbian, heterosexual—and cannot change. I have heard this claim made by heterosexual feminists who say that although the weight of *reason*, for them, is on the side of lesbianism, their *feelings* are irredeemably heterosexual. "Feelings" covers a lot here—these women mean to include such things as genital twinges and thumps, the presence or absence of guilt and fear and excitement, sexual and romantic fantasies, and so on. A woman who takes this position may claim that she cannot change the fact that she is sexually attracted only to men, which she experiences as a given, and so that she *cannot* take responsibility for her sexuality—that she is caught in a conflict between reason and feeling.

The peculiarity of this position, it seems to me, is the assumption that a woman has no influence over her own feelings, over her own sensual and emotive experience. Certainly some sexual habits, desires, fears, and the like have roots so deep that they are difficult, perhaps impossible, to change. But I believe that many women who want to experience lesbian sexuality in fact do reorient their feelings in terms of this desire; they teach themselves—usually, no doubt, with the help of other women—to have lesbian feelings. (They may or may not also teach themselves *not* to have heterosexual feelings; "crossdreaming," for example, occurs among both lesbians and heterosexuals.)

But the focus of a heterosexual woman who is moved by feminism to want to become lesbian need not be on changing her feelings, for one need not always behave as one feels. Feelings do not *require* expression—presumably everyone, on some occasions, chooses not to act on her feelings. So a woman whose only sexual feelings, as far as she knows, are heterosexual, but who believes that the weight of reason supports lesbianism, has good grounds for choosing not to follow her feelings but rather to refrain from participating in heterosexuality. She also has good reasons for making love with a woman, and if she does so, she may begin to have erotic feelings for her partner. I am reminded that one sort of advice for a bad mood is to start smiling, on the assumption that feelings follow behavior. Similarly, lesbian feelings may follow lesbian behavior.

It seems to me, then, that a woman who is not sexually aroused by women may nevertheless choose lesbian identity which, after all, includes a great deal more than sexuality. Regarding sexuality, such a woman may, perhaps temporarily, be a celibate lesbian, or she may want to participate in love-making with women even though she is not, or not much, sexually aroused. That a woman is erotically responsive to men but not to women does not limit her choices among lesbianism, heterosexuality, bisexuality, and celibate versions of these. In developing feminist reconstructions of sexuality, òne need not assume either that erotic feelings must be acted out in love-making or that love-making should occur only where there are erotic feelings.

Feelings by themselves are not definitive of sexual identity, and neither is the sex of one's sexual partners. Nevertheless, the latter has a central role. Some lesbians regularly engage in sexual intercourse with men (particularly, married lesbians and lesbian prostitutes), and some of these may never or rarely engage in sex with women; lesbian identity for these women depends on there being non-sexual reasons—typically economic—for continued heterosexual behavior. In the absence of such special reasons, regular heterosexual activity defeats the claim that one is a lesbian; such a woman would have instead to be identified as heterosexual or bisexual. Similarly, women who believe themselves to be heterosexual or bisexual but regularly engage in sexual activity only with women cannot, in the absence of special circumstances, sustain the claim of heterosexuality. Of course genital interaction with others is not essential to any of these identities: one may choose a celibate version (with or without masturbation) of any one of them.[4]

But what about a heterosexual feminist whose purported reason for engaging in heterosexual activity is just that she takes physical pleasure in it, physical pleasure she can experi-

---

[4] [In the nineties I am less contentious about labels for sexual orientation than I was when I wrote this essay.]

ence in no other way? It would be too great a sacrifice, she says, to give up this pleasure, even for the political and personal benefits she thinks would come from an identification other than heterosexual. In exploring this issue, it may turn out that the physical pleasure is not after all separable from the economic, emotional, social, and other advantages that she gains from heterosexual relationships. Such a woman may discover that her identification as heterosexual is not based primarily on genital pleasure as she had thought but, rather, on an understanding of the complex role that heterosexual activity plays in her life.

A woman who has such an understanding can correctly be said to be taking responsibility for her own sexuality, perhaps to be choosing heterosexuality, even though the inconsistency between her reason (lesbian) and her genital feelings and behavior (heterosexual) remains. For she has come to understand her heterosexual identity not as a fate irrevocably determined by genital sensations, but as a choice she has made on the basis of a variety of factors, a choice pushed upon her, to be sure, by the power of the institution of heterosexuality, but also one which she might not have made and might yet revoke. Indeed, as she comes to understand her sexuality in the process of taking responsibility for it, her sexual identity may itself change, for the process of discovery/creation dialectically transforms pre-existing reality.

It seems then that it does make sense to speak of all women—whatever our sexuality is and whatever it may become—as capable of taking responsibility for our sexuality, of discovering/creating our sexual orientation. If we define our own sexuality, we are more likely to be strong, self-creating, and independent women in many respects than if we accept the identity men impose upon us. Also, to take responsibility for sexuality requires study and thought about the meanings of different sexualities, and this consciousness-raising has important political implications. It means that there will be greater understanding among women of how patriarchy operates and also that there will be fewer heterosexuals, insofar as serious thought about heterosexuality leads women to withdraw from it. And taking responsibility for sexuality may contribute to a greater solidarity among women through a lessening of heterosexism and lesbophopia.

Let me focus briefly on this last idea, the connection between taking responsibility and overcoming lesbian oppression. Heterosexism is the conviction that heterosexuality is superior to other sexual identities, particularly as this conviction is held by those with the power to put their conviction into practice; it includes also the institutionalization of this supposed superiority, for example, in law and religion. A common form of heterosexism is what has been called "heterosexist solipsism," which is to behave as though everyone is heterosexual, ignoring the existence of other sexualities.

A woman who takes seriously the project of defining her own sexuality has to consider the possibility that she herself could be other than heterosexual; having done this, she is, I think, less likely to degrade lesbians and things lesbian. Also, taking responsibility for sexual identity raises consciousness about different sexualities and so makes women more aware of the fact that not everyone in their families, among their friends, and in their workplaces is heterosexual.

Lesbophobia, like heterosexism, may be lessened as one takes control of one's sexual identity. Some lesbophobia is fear of the unknown: lesbians seem threatening (to lesbians as well as non-lesbians) because one does not know what to expect from them; one may be afraid of being rejected or hurt or laughed at, or of not knowing how to act. Another kind of lesbophobia is fear of being or becoming one too. A woman thinking about choosing lesbianism for herself moves toward overcoming her lesbophobia in that she learns more about lesbians and, if she has the opportunity, may also get to know individual lesbians as lesbians; increased familiarity lessens the threat. Also, as a heterosexual woman taking responsibility thinks of herself as a potential lesbian, that possibility is likely to seem less frightening.

In taking responsibility for her own sexuality, a woman becomes more in charge of her own self, her own life, and so makes a crack in patriarchy. As women engage with one another about taking this responsibility, follow its implications in all areas of our lives, and have the courage to withstand the patriarchal forces that respond to our changes by attempting to push us back into subjugation, patriarchy loses its very meaning: for what is patriarchy without the guarantee to males that females are sexually available to them?

I appreciate help with this essay from members of SWIP, especially Anne Waters and Sandra Lee Bartky. For revisions, I am grateful for responses by students in several different classes.

For related discussion, consult Marilyn Frye's "Assignment: NWSA-Bloomington-1980: Speak on Lesbian Perspectives on Women's Studies," in Sinister Wisdom 14 (1980), *particularly pages 5-7.*

Hortense and Gladys on Sex

Hortense and Gladys came into being as I was recording my own thinking, the sort of thinking wherein one takes a position, questions it, gives an answer, questions again, and so on. As I wrote, the main contributors to the conversation began to seem continuously distinct, so they acquired names, and the writing took the form of dialogue.

The main voice is named Hortense. The first syllable of her name refers to her independence and capacity to see through nonsense, which I think of as whorish—whorish, that is, in the street-smart sense, not as whores are derogatorily stereotyped in polite patriarchy. The second syllable of her name refers to her intensity. Gladys, who keeps asking questions, tries to be cheerful and glad. While Hortense is an idealist who paddles about in the abstract, Gladys, a pragmatist, is more immersed in daily life.

Sometimes I think of the two voices as two parts of myself. At other times, I imagine them both as fictional: Hortense and Gladys, companions, lovers, talkers, with ideas always in process. And sometimes Gladys seems to be my real-life partner, or a friend, or someone I haven't met yet but might—and I am Hortense, explaining myself in response to Gladys's persistent questioning.

Hortense: Gladys, do you know that there is a *disorder* called "lack of interest in sex," so that if someone isn't interested in sex, she is supposed to need treatment, need to be changed? That idea has so influenced me that when you want to have sex and I don't, I'm inclined to feel that there's something wrong with *me*. But I think that your being interested in sex when I'm not requires an explanation just as much as my *not* being interested when you are.

Gladys: Yes, but you are hardly *ever* interested.

Hortense: Right. But if sex really is an invention of patriarchy, a tool men use as a means to keep women down, then my not being interested is appropriate; I *don't want* to be interested.

Gladys: I don't get it. People just *are* sexual. *Animals* are sexual. Sexuality comes with the species, like hunger, or playfulness.

Hortense: But why believe that? That's what they want us to believe. They tell us that just as they tell us that women "naturally" like to be fucked, and have babies, and take care of men. It's in their own interest.

Gladys: Well, sex *feels* natural. It feels like it comes from someplace deep in me, not from patriarchy.

Hortense: A testimony to the effectiveness of the system.

Gladys: I understand what you're saying, but I still want the closeness, the skin-on-skin. I *like* lovemaking, but you don't.

Hortense: Yes. I like my life, I'm absorbed in going about my business, and sex is an intrusion. Oh, I masturbate sometimes—usually without much interruption, while I'm reading or planning a lecture. But making love with someone else requires attention to the lovemaking.

Gladys: Yes. I *want* your attention.

Hortense: I give you attention in other ways, I—

Gladys: It's not the same—

Hortense: But I do think that relationships need sex; to know someone and have her know me, we need to be sexual together, to share sex. And you and I have done that. Unless we're into changing the sex, or changing ourselves through sex, why just do the same thing over and over? What comes of it?

Gladys: Well, maybe I would like to change what we do. We don't do it often enough to find out, because you don't want to.

Hortense: Right. I don't. I don't want to spend my energy that way. It's partly because I'm old. I've had so much sex, and I know more about sex and myself than I used to, and I know that time is short. I don't drink as much as I used to either. In both cases I want the energy for work, for politics, for other kinds of play.

Gladys: You're blocking. There is something that is *keeping* you from wanting sex, some block, some fear.

Hortense: You mean that there is something in my background that "explains" my values about sex? Yes, certainly; that's the way mainstream thinking works. What *doesn't* conform must have some explanation; what *does* conform doesn't need any. We're not supposed to question conformity.

Gladys: Still—

Hortense: Alright, maybe there is something in my past that illuminates my present values. How about this: Sex moves to opening and merging, to a return, some say, to the original oneness with mother. But my mother abandoned me psychically, emotionally, when I was an infant; she left me to scream and rage in my crib alone. So maybe I'm afraid of merging because I think it leads to being abandoned.

Gladys: But why expect women you know now to be like your mother?

Hortense: I'm not claiming that my attitude toward sex is reasonable because of its sources in my background—not at all. What makes it reasonable is its fit with my *politics*. It makes excellent political sense to refuse to participate in an institution that harms women and children and sustains hierarchies, whatever the emotional impetus for such refusal. But what about you? What explains your *liking* of sex?

Gladys: I just like it. The warmth, the closeness.

Hortense: Yes. You like it and I don't. Why should my attitude be traced to something in my past and yours not? Can't you tell a story about the roots of your liking sex?

Gladys: Well, I suppose it's the closeness I had with mother when I was little—I *didn't* get abandoned; I had warmth and merging, and I want that again.

Hortense: And your past experience doesn't count as "damage" whereas mine does because yours prepared you for the patriarchal system of sexuality, it tended to make you *like* sex.

Gladys: Wait a minute! I'm a lesbian! I've never had sex with a man. So why do you say that I was prepared for "the patriarchal system of sexuality"?

Hortense: The system doesn't have only heterosexuality in it. It can include same-sexuality, and is doing so more and more: think of how gay men are being assimilated now into the mainstream. Those gay boys are becoming real men!

Gladys: But lesbians violate heterosexuality and male domination in ways that gay men don't; we mock the principle that men have power over women.

Hortense: Yes, but most lesbians are still controlled by men in many ways, economically, politically—

Gladys: But lesbians can and do transform sex—sex can be *wonderful* between lesbians, and without hierarchy.

Hortense: Well, it certainly can be wonderful, and perhaps even without hierarchy. But if lesbians *could* transform the meaning of sex so that it wasn't fucking, so nobody got fucked—

Gladys: Some women *like* fucking.

Hortense: But think of what "fuck" means. One of the most hostile things you can say to someone is "fuck you." When I first realized that for most men, sex is fucking and that women are told it is "lovemaking" so as to get them/us to submit, I wondered why any female who realized this would willingly participate.

Gladys: For money?

Hortense: Apart from that. Being fucked and sucking— those are the ultimate degradations in patriarchy.

Gladys: Lots of people *like* being fucked and sucking.

Hortense: Yes, but at least partly because of the challenge, I would think; it's a challenge to show that you can do what others think will degrade you *without* feeling degraded, without feeling put down.

Gladys: Maybe, but—

Hortense: Meeting the challenge in this way doesn't change the social meaning of the behavior, but presupposes it. That lots of women and some men like to get fucked doesn't make "fuck you" a wish for a pleasureful day.

Gladys: Oh, Hortense, you just don't want to make love!

Hortense: Just so.

Decentering Sex

Lesbians are vastly unlike one another and (because we are a bit free from patriarchy) tend to be creative besides, so there are many different lesbian versions of everything we do, including sex. One lesbian version of sex is to have very little of it, or none at all: to move sex out of the center of one's life and toward the periphery.

Decentering sex may include masturbating, or no sexual activity at all, or occasional sexual activity with another or others. It may include having an intimate partner or partners, or not. It may mean little or no sex for one or several periods of one's life, or for a whole lifetime. And so on, through many variations.

As for reasons for decentering sex, some lesbians who do so have no conscious reasons at all. Others have stories of various complexity. Those who have been abused—sexually, physically, emotionally, spiritually—may explain wanting not to have sex primarily in terms of their experiences of abuse. Lesbian nuns may appeal to their vows. Some lesbians have political reasons for setting sex aside. Here I begin with a political approach.

Sexual desire and activity do not exist independently of culture but are made by human beings; they are constructed in mainstream cultures by men, who dominate those cultures.[1]

---

[1] The account I give here of connections among sex, gender, and domination is based mainly on Catharine MacKinnon's work in "Pleasure under Patriarchy" in *Theories of Human Sexuality*, edited by James H. Geer and

Sex is made by men through institutions that mold how people feel and act and think—including family, religion, education, science, media, the arts, fashion, and especially pornography (a point emphasized by Catharine MacKinnon). Sex is produced through the coercion of women and girls by men and boys, through humiliations and beatings and rapings and ever-present threats.

As I think of sex, then, it is not an elemental wild desire rooted deep in biology and layered over by culture; it is imposed upon me and I am tricked into feeling it as *though* it were me, from me, as though it were from inside me, came with me, came from me and not from them. Sexual desire is like an addict's desire for her drug: deep, bodily, but imposed from outside by those who profit from it.

As sex does not pre-exist culture so, I believe, females and males do not pre-exist sex but are postulated as pre-existing from within the sex system. Sex itself engenders human beings—that is, gives human beings gender—making humans either females and then women, or males and then men, except where resistance interferes with the process. Male domination is thus built in: to be a woman is to be subordinate to men; to be a man is to have power over women. (So some lesbians refuse to be women and spell the word differently.) Female and male, woman and man, are all defined and constructed so as to guarantee the domination of women by men.

William T. O'Donohue (New York: Plenum Press, 1987); *Feminism Unmodified: Discourses on Life and Law* (Cambridge, Mass.: Harvard University Press, 1987); and *Toward a Feminist Theory of the State* (Cambridge, Mass.: Harvard University Press, 1989).

I have been inspired also by the work of Melinda Vadas, for example, her article "The Pornography/Civil Rights Ordinance v. The BOG: And the Winner Is. . . ?" in *Hypatia* 7, no. 3 (Summer 1992); 94-109. Note also "Sex Resistance in Heterosexual Arrangements" by A Southern Women's Writing Collective, in *The Sexual Liberals and the Attack on Feminism*, edited by Dorchen Leidholdt and Janice G. Raymond (New York: Pergamon Press, 1990).

The core of the concept of woman, that which guarantees male domination, is the stipulation that to be a woman is, centrally, to be rapable. To be rapable means both to be capable of being raped, and to "deserve" to be raped. Men argue about whom they are entitled to rape—their wives, for example? Women who sexually excite them? Prostitutes? The women of an "enemy" village? Most men agree, though, that every man is entitled to rape at least some women.

For a while I thought that fuckability was perhaps more significant than rapability in the construction of women because within the system fuckability is entirely "normal." Then I remembered that wimmin speak of fucking one another, and that in some heterosexual settings "fuck" is used synonymously with "have sex" so both women and men can be said to be fuckable. (Twenty years ago "fuck" was an asymmetrical verb [if he fucked her, it did not follow that she fucked him] but it has become, or is in the process of becoming, a symmetrical verb [if he fucks her, then she fucks him]. This apparent change in the meaning of "fuck" has occurred, I suppose, in response to the women's movement. It is a response that some—including me—may deplore, for it masks the fact that in fucking, men establish and maintain the subjugation of women.[2])

In any case, the concept of fuckability does not capture the significance of woman's non-consent. That women can be fucked when they/we do not consent—that is, that women are rapable—is the foundation of male power over women as women. As Melinda Vadas puts it, women are rapable "because it is necessarily the case that our consent is accidental to the identity of a sex act as such."[3] In other words: What sex *is* requires that sex be completely independent of whether the

---

[2] For discussion of the earlier, non-symmetrical usage, consult "'Pricks' and 'Chicks': A Plea for 'Persons'" by Robert Baker, in *Sexist Language: A Modern Philosophical Analysis*, edited by Mary Vetterling-Braggin (no place: Littlefield, Adams & Co., 1981).

[3] Correspondence, September 20, 1992.

woman consents to it. The nature, the definition, the essence of sex requires that sex be enacted upon creatures whose consent, while perhaps legally or socially or emotionally important in particular cases, is explicitly excluded from the conditions for its existence.

So in writing about sex as constructing women as dominated by men, I say that sex makes women rapable. At the same time, it makes men rapists. Sex, then, subjugates women not because it just happens to be a handy tool for keeping women down, not because it was lying about in nature/culture and men just picked it up to use for their own purposes. On the contrary. As a form of life, a source of feeling, a way of behaving and relating, sex is in its very structure and substance a means whereby men exercise power over women. To remove this aspect of sex—to try to cleanse it or purge it or reform it—would be to eliminate sex itself.

But what about lesbian sex? In the context of an analysis of sex as the centerpole of the cultural apparatus that subjugates women to men, is lesbian sex just one of several kinds of sex, and so part of the system? Or is it to be contrasted with the dominant system and so, perhaps, not sex at all? Marilyn Frye writes,

> [T]he term "sex" is an inappropriate term for what lesbians do. . . . [W]e should adopt a very wide and general concept of "doing it." Let it be an open, generous, commodious concept encompassing all the acts and activities by which we generate with each other pleasures and thrills, tenderness and ecstasy, passages of passionate carnality of whatever duration or profundity. Everything from vanilla to licorice, from puce to chartreuse, from velvet to ice, from cuddles to cunts, from chortles to tears. . . .[4]

---

[4] Marilyn Frye, "Lesbian 'Sex'" in *Lesbian Philosophies and Cultures*, edited by Jeffner Allen (Albany, N.Y.: State University of New York Press, 1990), 305, 313-14.

Claudia Card argues that because having sex is connected with reproduction, and lesbian love-making is not, "'having sex' is a phallic concept that cannot be applied without distortion to lesbian love-making."[5]

My notion is that the heart of sex is male genital arousal and orgasm and that by extension "sex" is an appropriate name for female genital arousal and orgasm. (The institution of sex might be called "genitalism" to indicate the emphasis and value placed on genital activity in patriarchy.) So I say that lesbians do have sex, although much that lesbians do in intimate relationships is not sex. The question is, then, in the light of an analysis of the sort sketched here, does lesbian sex, by virtue of being sex, participate in the subjugation of women by men?

Catharine MacKinnon says that when women have sex with women and not with men, "women's sexuality remains constructed under conditions of male supremacy; women remain socially defined as women in relation to men; [and] the definition of women as men's inferiors remains sexual even if not heterosexual, whether men are present at the time or not."[6] Notice that she speaks here as a man, not from a deliberately wimmin's space. In wimmin's space, the conditions of male supremacy are at least partly negated; wimmin define ourselves in relation to wimmin and without reference to men; and wimmin are *not* defined as men's inferiors.

Still, getting out from under male domination is not just a matter of living and thinking in wimmin's space. We cannot separate ourselves from patriarchy so easily. One might as well argue that bringing meat to a vegetarian potluck supper makes the meat a vegetarian dish because it is prepared and presented and eaten in vegetarian space. A vegetarian environment doesn't change the meat enough—it doesn't get it far

---

[5] Claudia Card, "Intimacy and Responsibility: What Lesbians Do" in *At the Boundaries of Law: Feminism and Legal Theory*, edited by Martha Albertson Fineman and Nancy Sweet Thomadsen (New York: Routledge, 1991), 89.
[6] *Toward a Feminist Theory of the State, ibid.*, (consult note 1), 141-42.

enough away from the dominant environment—to keep it from being meat. Similarly, that sex occurs between wimmin doesn't change sex enough to keep it from being sex.[7]

Lesbian sex exists in an environment of male domination constructed by heterosexuality and so, it seems to me, cannot escape being part of that system, just by virtue of being between or among only wimmin. The very existence of sex between wimmin exemplifies and shores up the patriarchal idea that sex is of value. Further, insofar as sex is a major focus of lesbian culture, lesbian culture supports the patriarchal ideology that sex should be central to culture and to life.

I do think that particular sexual interactions between wimmin may be more or less separate from patriarchy in terms of the experiences of the wimmin involved. For one thing, wimmin can probably change and negotiate power in sexual relationships more freely than heterosexual couples can. In heterosexuality, although who does what to whom can vary widely, *whatever* happens tends to be an expression of male power. "He did it to her" and "she did it to him" both usually refer to manifestations of his power over her. In contrast, when only females are involved, anything that takes place may make either (or any) female dominant. In sex between (or among) females, whether a particular woman has the preponderance of power may change from partner to partner, from episode to episode, even from moment to moment. Although some lesbians see to it that in virtually all their relationships they are dominant and some lesbians prefer always to be submissive, lesbian sex is probably more open and flexible with respect to power than heterosexuality is.

---

[7] But perhaps it could do so. It the entire system of human food and of how meat comes to be eaten were different, meat might be "vegetarian" in the sense that eating it would be consistent with respect for nonhuman animals, for the worldwide food economy, and for health, and so consistent with vegetarianism. If the entire system of human interaction were different, "sex" might be consistent with the absence of even the concept of hierarchy.

But heterosexism and sexism are often present in lesbian sexual interactions, sometimes when one woman is or pretends to be masculine and another feminine, sometimes in assumptions, feelings, fantasies, and the like. Also, lesbian sex is surrounded and frequently permeated by systems such as racism and classism that provide their own power dynamics, defining some women as more powerful than others. So while I think that particular lesbian sexual relationships may to some degree escape the dominant power dynamic, I think also that sex between wimmin does involve men's power over women both in being yet another instantiation of and so support for the system that creates gender power and in manifesting aspects of power-over.

The question remains whether power-over *must* be present in sex. Suppose that no sex occurred anywhere for a long period of time except lesbian sex. How would sex change? Would genital activity cease to be sex? Or would it, perhaps, disappear in favor of non-genital ways of behaving? That's an experiment I'd like to be around for.

Meanwhile, I choose to set sex aside for now or, rather, to make it peripheral to my life and values. I want to be rid, of course, of the whole sex system, including the genital, the genders, and the hierarchies. But I can't just set all that aside, whereas I can put genital activity itself in a peripheral place in my life. I do so largely because under present conditions, it seems to me, to have sex is to cooperate with the male-dominant reality it constructs.

I make this choice in accord with the analysis sketched earlier. But what inspires me to accept this analysis? First, age is important in several ways. I am nearing sixty. Because I have done a lot of sex in my life, sex of many kinds and with many kinds of people, curiosity no longer drives me. Because I no longer live in a world where sexual liaisons seem to offer the best or only opportunity for a stylish and exciting life, for intimacy, for a meaningful identity, the social context in which I live no longer motivates me to sex. Because I am strongly aware of the limited number of years left to me to accomplish what I set out to do in my life (i.e., figure out a few things in writing), I choose against using (much) time and energy in sex. Finally, because the skin of my genitals is thin and brittle so that any touch must be gentle if it is not to be painful, I am inclined to avoid the risk of physically hurting.

Past sexual experience is also a factor in my wanting to set sex aside. The heterosexual abuse I have suffered as an adult, including being raped and beaten and having to pretend pleasure, supports the analysis of sex as men's main way of controlling women, and so as something I don't want in a central place in my life. Probably I am also influenced by having been sexually abused as a child, although I don't seem to have memories of that.

But my sexual experience has not been all bad. I have participated in lovemaking (with women, alone, long ago with men) that has been fun, or deeply satisfying, or in one way or another amazing. I don't think it can reasonably be said that "what I need is good experience." Still, my memories of the good experiences don't overcome my resistance, just as a vegetarian's memories of steak dinners that she once found delicious do not overcome her resistance to eating meat now, knowing what she knows.

For the time being at least, I find affection and love, closeness and intimacy, fun and excitement, identity and meaning—and emergence if I can stand it—(mostly) independent of sex. I also honor other wimmin's choosing differently.

VALUE

Lesbian Feminism in Process

Twenty years ago, many new lesbians in the u.s. came out into a developing radical lesbian feminist movement. Today, new lesbians are more likely to come out into a gay or queer movement dominated by men who tell them that they belong there and who tend to ignore or trivialize feminism. Some new dykes, I am told, refuse the name "lesbian" (choosing "gay" or "queer" instead) because "lesbians are feminists and I'm not a feminist."[1] How much do these wimmin know about lesbian feminism?[2]

Unlike cultures that pass values on to new generations through explicit teaching in families and schools, lesbian feminism has few if any structures intended to transmit ideas to newcomers. Many of the classical texts are out of print. Current resources are not widely available and, in any case, they tend to assume rather than explicate fundamental ideas. When lesbian feminists and other dykes get together, the situation often does not foster careful discussion of values. So it's worth saying here something about basic lesbian feminist ideas.

For many feminist lesbians, coming out was inspired not only by love of wimmin but by political analyses of heterosexuality as oppressive to women. In contrast, for the lesbian, gay, and bisexual movement, the pattern is often reversed:

---

[1] Observation by Virginia Ingram.

[2] Some wimmin whose values and beliefs seem to me to be lesbian feminist reject "lesbian" (too bland) or "feminist" (too heterosexual). I do not mean to exclude them by using the name "lesbian feminist."

rather than politics inspiring sexual orientation, one first discovers that one has a sexual orientation unacceptable to the mainstream and then becomes political. Queer is different from both in that many young queers seem to develop political awareness and ways of transgressing sexual and gender boundaries at the same time.

Lesbian feminism has obviously influenced the gay and queer movements, and conversely. In addition, lesbian feminism has evolved over the years because its creators have grown older, because of outside changes, and in response to specific criticisms. Responding to criticism of the desire for "purity," for example, some feminist lesbians are now less judgmental toward ourselves and others than we used to be, less inclined to insist that wimmin "should" hold certain beliefs and live in certain ways.[3] Anti-racist criticism has been important too; for example, some white separatists have become more supportive of lesbians of color choosing to do political work with men from their communities of origin.

It would be worth tracing the evolution of lesbian feminism in detail.[4] Here, however, I can only explicate—briefly— my current versions of three ideas: separating from men; rejecting the family; and lesbianism as involving choice. I write especially for lesbians who are unfamiliar with these ideas.

SEPARATING FROM MEN

Like all of my dyke ideas, separating, conceived abstractly, is embedded in commitment to change, specifically a commitment to the elimination of hierarchies, including hierarchies

[3] The desire for purity is connected with a desire for perfection that some wimmin have because of how badly we've been mistreated. In my own case, I still love what is pristine, but now am likely to exercise this taste in aesthetics more than politics.

[4] A partial herstory of ideas is provided by Carol Anne Douglas in *Love and Politics: Radical Feminist and Lesbian Theories* (San Francisco: ism press, inc., 1990).

of race, class, culture, gender, ability, appearance, and sexual orientation. Separating creates change partly through influencing what is outside of it, but mainly in inspiring dykes to create our own worlds: politically, materially, socially, philosophically, spiritually. At present few if any separating wimmin escape entirely from male-dominant society, but separating can provide, I think, the broadest possible field on which to build our own ways of life.

Separating for me means in part that I stay away from men and ignore them as much as I can. I do so because I am interested in wimmin and care about us, because I like many wimmin and love some, because I think that only with wimmin can I do anything worthwhile in life, because only with wimmin does my life make sense and feel good.

I keep away from males also because they remind me of rapes and beatings and humiliation, of domination and exploitation; because men, having had lives fundamentally different from mine, can't understand me; because I find most men ugly or arrogant or both; because I don't trust most men; and because most men, being to some degree misogynists or lesbophobes or both, dislike me and other wimmin. With effort, I might find men who are exceptions to these generalizations. But I have reason not to make the effort. Males already get more than their fair share of goods of every kind compared to females of the same race and class. To search out men who are exceptions exacerbates the inequality by giving them even more attention than they get already. Far better to take from men (and/or give them nothing) and to share what one can with wimmin/women.

Sometimes I do need to deal with a particular male—a colleague, a repair man, a clerk in a store, a neighbor. I interact with these men for reasons that are specific to the individuals and the occasions. The exchanges are always brief and sometimes barely cordial.

I have not always had the privilege of restricting my interactions with men to such an extent. For years, my income depended partly on my relating to males (for example, by talk-

ing philosophy with colleagues). Also, before and into the seventies my self-esteem depended largely on men's opinions of
me.

It is much harder to separate from men's products than
from individual men. I rarely read men's books unless I am
after specific information, as from a dictionary. I rarely listen to
men's music. I do listen to radio talk and watch television
news and read daily newspapers not only for information and
self-protection but also for entertainment and escape, a practice
I'd like to be free of. And most of the material objects I use
every day—house and car and computer—are from men.

Other wimmin who separate from men do so differently.
Some make exceptions for particular family members or
friends. Some make exceptions for doing political work in
coalition with men. Some never speak to men at all. Some eat
wimmin-grown food and live in wimmin-made houses. And
so on. There are many versions of separating, all of which deny
attention and energy to men and give it instead to wimmin.

Some wimmin think separating is unrealistic because
"there will always be men in the world." But for me, separating as such is not the elimination of men from *the* world, but
rather from *this* world, or *our* world, or *my* world. Separating
creates relatively male-free, female-focused spaces. Some think
of such worlds as interim refuges, places where they can go to
rest and to gain strength and inspiration for a return to the
mainstream. I think of them mainly as realizations of lesbian
feminist politics: not as preparations for political work but as
its location. For me, wimmin's spaces are places for struggles
around race and class and culture; sites for the development of
dyke economic, social, and cultural institutions; and arenas
for identifying, capturing, and killing the devils of men's
dominion.

REJECTING THE FAMILY

Many radical feminist dykes reject the institution of the
family because, while family systems differ among cultures,

most have gender and age hierarchies built into them: males over females, adults over children and, in some cases, young and middle-aged adults over old people. Families are designed to transmit and enforce these hierarchies. In many cases they do so partly through terrorism. Women and children and old people are abused emotionally, sexually, physically, and spiritually. Family structure enables this abuse by legitimating power-over relationships and by hiding the abuse from outsiders and often even from family members themselves. All patriarchal families are based on domination and have at their core the subjugation—sometimes to the point of torture and beyond—of less powerful members.

I object to family also because membership is not wholly voluntary. Except for her partner (and perhaps adopted or foster children), a family member doesn't get to choose her relatives. As a young woman, I used to rail against having to deal with my parents who were, I would say to myself, definitely not people I would want to see again should I meet them at a party. Even now it seems bizarre to me that one is *given* one's parents, grandparents, siblings, aunts and uncles, and so on, and that one is typically expected to spend time with these unchosen relatives, probably to be nice to them, perhaps even to like or love them. What if your interests are so different you can't get beyond small talk? What if you don't like them or they don't like you or both? What if when you are together, you—perhaps all of you—end up anxious or angry or bored? Why, in such circumstances, should you use your energies being with your family?

Some would answer: for security. Your family will always be there for you, take care of you—or, at least, let you in. Not all families follow these rules, of course, especially with dyke daughters. Still, it makes sense for some wimmin—those who value a sense of security that only their family of origin can provide or, perhaps, those expecting a significant inheritance—to maintain contact.

Because family is so far from my lesbian values, I am still shocked when lesbians marry. To have a lesbian "wedding" seems to me to violate part of lesbianism's value: freedom from marriage and family. Giving birth is also not part of my lesbian world. I think that, as things are now, dyke energies are so much needed for making dyke cultures and for getting patriarchy off and out of us that it's fine if the youngest dyke generation consists just of girls or teenagers discovering/creating themselves as dykes. I can get along very well without any infants or small children at all. I know that some lesbians, though, do want to live with babies; I would like it if those who decide to do so choose not to give birth themselves but find a way to get around the considerable obstacles to lesbians adopting or otherwise taking in children, and share their homes with a girl or girls who need the care the lesbians will provide.[5]

I could go on. Sex, both forced and consensual, is of course central to families; but I want to decenter sex. Families, because they impose obligations, are hotbeds of guilt; but I want to be rid of guilt. And so on. I have many reasons for wanting to be family-free, reasons that are bathed in experiences of pain suffered in my own family of origin, a family that was not an aberration but an ordinary expression of patriarchy and so of the oppression of women and little girls.

I am offended by the use of the term "family" by dykes who think in positive ways about "gay and lesbian families." By using the word "family" positively, they rub out my experiences and those of the many other wimmin who have been badly hurt or worse in their families. Besides, I think that if lesbians use the word "family" for our own groupings, we may be sucked back unaware into mainstream patterns. Refusing to use the term "family" for dykes together may be a reminder of the importance of finding new ways to live.

CHOOSING LESBIANISM

Lesbianism is often, I believe, at least partly a matter of choice. But lesbianism as a choice is being denied in the current

---

[5] Thanks to Marcia Levin.

push for lesbian, gay, and bisexual civil rights, a context in which it is widely held that "sexual orientation" is not chosen but innate. Hence, it is argued, one cannot change one's "sexual orientation" and so should not be penalized for it.

If persuading the mainstream that lesbianism is "innate" serves the long-term interest of lesbians better than available alternatives, as in some situations it may, it is nevertheless important, in my opinion, to keep alive at least among dykes other ways of thinking. For some dykes, the idea that lesbianism is a biological given harmonizes with their experiences. But others find, as I do, that a biological account is inconsistent with their sense of having chosen and continuing to choose wimmin and with their commitment to defining their own identities.

Moreover, the genetic-origins account of lesbianism is politically dangerous. Its political purpose is partly to discourage heterosexual women from coming out; if heterosexual women believe that they have no choice, many of those who otherwise would decide to be dykes are likely to keep on trying to get along as heterosexual, thus helping to ensure that most men have girl friends or wives most of the time. In the dominant power system it's important for males to have females to subordinate and to use as targets for their anger and violence because without women, men are likely to direct their energies instead against the corporate-military-government system that exploits them: they might make revolution. In addition to keeping powerless men occupied (women are much like football and drugs in this respect), defining lesbianism as biological also lays the foundation for scientific attempts to prevent or "cure" lesbianism and for scientific "justifications" for incarcerating or killing us.

For me, lesbianism is a way of life—many ways of life—whose various aspects do not follow from some nugget of "sexual preference" but which are themselves developed and woven together by each womon. Lesbianism involves relationships with lovers and others; the sorts of activities, including work, that one engages in; politics, spirituality, sense of beauty, personal style, and so on. Choice has a role in all these aspects of lesbian life. Coming out to others—with whom, when, how, how much—is also for many wimmin a matter for continuing decision and choice. To shrink lesbianism to a kernel of "sexual orientation," whether that is taken to be given by biology or by early experience or chosen in love and politics, is to me a gross distortion.

In an earlier writing I speak of a womon's coming out to herself as a process of "discovery/creation."[6] Sometimes, I say there (trying to wrench lesbian reality out of male language), a woman coming out may feel that she is *discovering* that she is a lesbian (and perhaps that she always has been, or in some ways always has been); sometimes a womon coming out experiences herself as *creating* herself and her life as a lesbian; often, I suggest, wimmin experience their lesbianism as both discovery and creation. I take each womon's lesbianism to be whatever she says it is—a discovery, a creation, both, or something else. The important thing to me is that *she* gets to decide.

As lesbian cultures develop, perhaps a single term will be agreed upon to encompass the whole range of experiences of coming out. Certainly the idea of lesbians choosing, of lesbians as agents, of lesbians as creating value, has become more central for lesbian feminists in the last decade or so.[7] In addition, dyke scientists, I believe, are in the process of construing the realm of the biological so that rather than being a means to control us it supports our freedom.

I deliberately resist the inclination to think that all dykes "should" adopt these ideas. Nor do I wish that they would do so. It's okay with me that some lesbians decide they are comfortable enough with men to do political work with them; that some lesbians find so much of value in the institution of the

[6] "Taking Responsibility for Sexuality," this volume, p. 102.
[7] Thanks partly to the work of Sarah Lucia Hoagland in *Lesbian Ethics: Toward New Value* (Palo Alto, Calif.: Institute for Lesbian Studies, 1988).

family that they choose to form lesbian families and experiment with reforms; and that some lesbians feel their lesbianism so deeply and thoroughly that they come to the conclusion that they can define it only as innate. I hope that these choices *are* choices, and that they benefit the wimmin who make them and others of us as well.

I don't want all dykes to have the values I have, but I don't want to be alone in holding them, either. Nor do I want them to disappear when old lesbian feminists die.

On the Edge

To be marginal, on the edge, over the edge, to drop out; to prove I can get in and then quit; to stay in for the money, moving ever edgeward—

Many years later my mother Angela would still chastise me, "You wanted to be editor of the high school paper and you got the job and then you didn't want to do it, you wanted to join a sorority and you got in and then you got yourself kicked out, you—"

She was right about the facts. I've noticed it myself. There's precious little invented by other people that I want to be part of for very long. That was true when I was young and it's still true. Get in to prove I can do it, get out. Get in to find out what's going on, figure it out, get out. Or get in, and if I have to stay (usually for the money), slide out to the periphery and cling to the edge.

So what's going on?

I want to make my own—what to say?—not my own *world* (something less than that, I don't get to decide everything) . And not my own *interpretation* (something more than that, I can bring some things in and out of existence). And not quite my own *world-"view,"* it's not vision only; perhaps my own *world-picture*, pictures are not just visual but can be conceptual, tactile, even aural—. Or I could focus on words: my own

world-account, world-description, world-story? My own
world-compression. A way of compressing all the swirls into a
form, an emotionally intelligible—

My own beliefs and values. I need to make my own beliefs
and values.

Doesn't everybody? It has always felt entirely ordinary to me
to want not to be a beginner in established, ongoing worlds, to
want not to live by rules and customs made by other people, to
resist situations in which others determine the conditions of
my life—

Entirely ordinary. Every new generation does it. Young dykes,
for example, don't want to be what old dykes were at their
age. Young dykes make new styles and attitudes, new ways of
being—glorious.

Dykes *especially* cannot be expected to live in worlds made by
others. A commitment to being a dyke is partly a commitment
to invention—a commitment to making up one's own world,
or parts of it, anyway.

But not alone, even for solitaries like me. Ideas about what's
going on and what I want have their sources in memory, imag-
ination, interactions, especially in interactions with what other
dykes make—art, events, communities—and in interactions
with dykes face-to-face, and with crowds of dykes. (And in
interactions with patriarchy, too.)

Patterns of overlapping circles, one circle for each dyke: Some
of my ideas are only mine, many overlap with those of other
dykes, some are shared by nearly all dykes. (Some overlap
with the ideas of non-dykes; I won't live long enough to
rethink, refeel, everything, although I would like to be able to
"finish" the story.)

So here's how it is. However wonderful a group or organization or community might be, I cannot live comfortably in it unless I am part of creating its center, of making its rules and customs, of making policy decisions and daily decisions. If I am not part of the creating process, I establish myself on an edge, taking privileges as I can get them, perhaps making reformist forays inward, but always moving back to the periphery where I build as I can my own place or, if there are other lovers of the edge with values like mine, where together we make for ourselves a place on the edge. Such a place—such a palace—if it's far out enough, and although it's constrained by its attachments to the dominant structure, has lots of space for self-direction.

So it was with the women's studies program I lived in for nearly two decades. I helped found and sustain it and was always close to what went on within it. For the university, the program was an annoying blister on the margin; for me, for us, it was a protective bubble full of wimmin and ideas and relative freedom, perched on the edge.

Soon I'll retire. I'll leave the university then, and probably move west. I expect more balancing acts—and I'd like to learn Chinese.

NOTES ON WORDS
ACKNOWLEDGMENTS

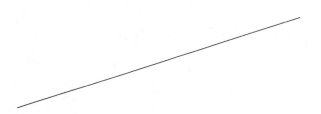

NOTES ON WORDS

The language that comes most readily to my mind sometimes embodies values I reject. For example, I might hear in my head "this assumption raises three questions" and then notice the phallic implications of "raises." Or I might automatically think "that way of talking denigrates women" and then, recognizing the racism ("to denigrate" means "to blacken"), rethink what I mean. Such editing comes from the intention of making political change; its value may be as much in the consciousness it requires as in the fact that it keeps certain expressions from being used.

Although I have tried to attend to the various meanings of the words I have used in this book, there no doubt remain expressions that I would eliminate if I were aware of all their implications. Also, in some cases, I have decided to leave questionable (but never, as far as I know, insulting or offensive) terminology in the text for the sake of clarity or emphasis or flow.

Here (in alphabetical order) are some of the sorts of terms I try to avoid, especially in the later writings.

Ableist. Vision is the privileged sense in mainstream thought. A philosophy is a "world-view," a good idea is an "insight," and ignorance is "blindness"; one's opinion is one's "view" or "viewpoint" or "perspective," and if one comprehends something, one may remark, "Yes, I see." I dislike such epistemological uses of vision metaphors both because they tend to ignore the experiences of people who are blind and because I don't want to be pulled, without conscious decision, into a metaphysics that makes the main relationship between people and things one of sight. So I use these terms only occasionally.

I also mean to edit out of my words such ableist expressions as "lame duck" and "they were deaf to her entreaties," as well as, for example, those that refer to running or walking as if no one were wheeling, and those that imply that people who are intellectually quick are more valuable than those who are or appear to be slow.

Out of respect for little people, I have also eliminated "to belittle."

Capitalist. The commodification of daily life means that the language of buying and selling is often applied metaphorically. So one might think of "the cost of coming out," or of "paying attention," or, referring to the conclusion of a discussion, of "the bottom line." I would rather find less profit-oriented ways of thinking.

Also, I have been struck by my tendency to emphasize my "ownership" of ideas and actions by writing, for example, not merely "my decisions" but "my *own* decisions," not merely "my values" but "my *own* values." Some of these "owns" are still in the text for emphasis; but mostly I have found other ways to say what I mean.

Christian. I avoid "crucial" and "crux" because these terms may convey, if only at an unconscious level, images of "the" (not merely "a") cross, which I certainly want not to do when my subject is something else.

Heterosexist. "Straight" has a long history of at least superficially commendatory uses: "He's straight in his business dealings," "the straight and narrow," "they want a straight answer." So when "straight" is used to mean "heterosexual," it leans toward the heterosexist, to my mind. Certainly some heterosexuals use it of themselves with the implication that their "straightness" makes them superior. So I don't use "straight" to mean "heterosexual."

Hierarchical. I try to avoid gratuitous comparisons. Several years ago, a student who spent lots of time with small children and thought a lot about how to keep them from falling into the conceptual pits of patriarchy would remind our women's studies class not to make hierarchies without good reason; every time one of us would unthinkingly refer to what was better or worse, more or less important, more or less valuable there would be a stir from her.[1] Partly because of these reminders, I became super-conscious of how often I was inclined to give "grades," to make rankings, without good reason for doing so. I already knew that thinking about who is "more oppressed" is detrimental to working against oppression; I began learning then that comparative thinking in other contexts also often (not always) supports divisiveness, competition, and feelings of superiority and inferiority. So generally I choose not to think about, for example, whether it is "harder" to be a lesbian in one place or time than another, whether one piece of writing is "better" than another, or which are my "most important" values. Consciously limiting comparative thinking has not only enabled me to make fewer gratuitous judgments, it also has sometimes prodded me to find new (I won't say "better") descriptions.

A different sort of hierarchical concept that I tend to avoid is *understanding.* I do not like the (Platonic) notion that to have a clear grasp of an idea is to *stand under* it; I don't believe that ideas are superior to people or that they exist separately from people. Instead of "understand," I often (but not always) use terms such as "comprehend," "grasp," and "appreciate."

Militaristic. Dyke struggles may sometimes benefit from being construed as war—tactics and strategy, fighting, battles, victory and defeat. But I generally prefer other ways of thinking.

I also want not to use the language of weapons metaphorically. I don't say "take a shot at it" (for "take a chance") or

---

[1] Thanks to Jeni Snyder.

"upshot" (which is phallic as well as violence-related) or "What is the target date?" or "What are you aiming at?" I don't want shots and targets and aiming to be so ordinary, so unremarkable.

Phallic. Phallic language, insidiously snaking its way into seemingly woman-centered discussions, can reinforce phallic imprinting, I believe. But phallic images are so pervasive and tenacious that even after nearly a quarter-century of trying to purge myself of them, I may find myself about to write, for example, "hard questions come up" or even "the upsurge of the women's movement."

I also dislike "project" (as in "the students are working on their projects") and "point" (as in "the main point is . . ."). "To project" comes from "to throw forward"—what could be more phallic than that? A pointing finger, perhaps? Still, I find it difficult to be rid of the these terms.

Racist and anti-Semitic. I have recently heard people say that a doting mother is "a Jewish mother," that a room where clothes are drying looks like "a Chinese laundry," and that rambunctious children are "wild Indians." In addition to rejecting such obvious uses of anti-Semitic and racist stereotypes, I also avoid evaluative uses of terms such as "black," "white," "yellow," "kinky," and so on.

I have also eliminated "evil" from my writing (if not yet from my thought), thanks partly to a remark from a Jewish lesbian colleague, who told me that my use of this christian term was offensive to her as a Jew.[2]

Here are some additional matters concerning my use of language.

Capitalization. When I want not to contribute to the oppressiveness of some mainstream entity (christianity, the english language, the united states), I usually do not capitalize its name. But when I am writing in a consciously patriarchal voice

---

[2] Thanks to Bette Tallen.

or, more often, when it seems to me that the absence of an expected initial capital letter is likely to distract from what I am saying, I generally follow the rules I was brought up with.

Plurals. Whenever I can I try to use plurals rather than abstract nouns to refer to, for example, *liberations, energies, feminisms, oppressions,* (political) *movements.* The purpose is to tie the discourse to the actual plurality of the phenomena. In the same spirit, I often prefer to speak of women rather than "woman" and "families" rather than "the family." But there are some contexts in which an abstract noun is required: I oppose (the institution of) the family, not (particular) families.

"We." It is standard academic style to use "we," "us," and "our" not merely to create connection between writer and readers ("We turn now to . . ."; "Let us consider . . .") but also to suck readers into the values of the writer without warning. So writers say "we value," "we want," "we know," and "our culture." I choose not to use a plural pronoun in such a way unless I am fairly sure that the claim holds true of everyone who might be in the audience.

Wimmin. Women (singular, woman) are defined by men, whereas wimmin (singular, womon), seek to define ourselves. My choice of which spellings to use depends on whose ideas I am representing. In the more recent writings in this collection, when I refer to adult females from patriarchal contexts, I use patriarchal spellings; when I am speaking of or in dyke contexts, the spellings show that.

Wimmin are also women (I assume that none escape patriarchy entirely), but some women, perhaps, are never wimmin—never try to define themselves—and some may not have even a potential to be wimmin. Still, I like to think of the two sets of spellings as referring to different contexts in which females are described, not to different types or categories of females. This approach is a matter of faith that all females can at some time get free enough of patriarchy to at least partly define themselves.

In these comments I am just nibbling at the edges of english. I haven't even touched on sexism and heterosexism in language or how, for example, the built-in dualisms (female-male, black-white, emotion-reason, nature-culture, etc.) embody domination. But readers of this book are likely to be aware that english and other dominant-culture languages degrade and make invisible oppressed peoples; that they mask the agency of white males in creating and sustaining oppressions; and that they often provide virtually no way for subjugated people to say some of what we are feeling and thinking.[3]

---

[3] For detailed discussion of how english constructs patriarchy, consult *Speaking Freely: Unlearning the Lies of the Fathers' Tongues* by Julia Penelope (New York: Pergamon Press, 1990).

I appreciate also Sarah Lucia Hoagland's care with language in *Lesbian Ethics: Toward New Value* (Palo Alto, Calif.: Institute of Lesbian Studies, 1988). For example, she always refers to wimmin by their complete names, never, in the (originally British) male fashion, by surnames only; I follow her in this practice.

ACKNOWLEDGMENTS

I thank Jeffner Allen, editor of the series of which the book is a part, for her careful and insightful readings of the manuscript, her consistent patience and support, and her friendship.

I thank Lois Patton, Editor-in-Chief at SUNY Press, for her confidence in this work and for her patience.

I thank Helen Power, whose superb leadership of the Women's Studies Program at Washington University made it possible for me to go on leave and complete this manuscript; Karen Kiske-Zimmerman, whose support as Administrative Assistant to the Women's Studies Program helped me immensely to accomplish this writing; and colleagues and administrators at the University who, for years, left me alone to do my work.

I thank Kathryn Brooks for saying, years ago in Albuquerque, that this book was needed.

I thank Ryn Edwards, who read and commented in detail on an early version of the manuscript and from time to time tells me of her students' responses to parts of it that she uses in her classes.

I thank the members of Midwestern SWIP (Society for Women in Philosophy) who attended meetings during the 1970s and 1980s when I did; being with them two or three weekends a year made it possible for me to go on. I appreciate especially the work and presence of SWIP members Claudia Card, Jacquelyn Zita, María Lugones, Marilyn Frye, Sandra Bartky, and Sarah Lucia Hoagland.

I thank Fox for editing and producing the journal *Lesbian Ethics*; Azizah al-Hibri, Peg Simons, and Linda Lopez McAlister for editing *Hypatia: A Journal of Feminist Philosophy*; and Marjorie Larney for Acacia Books.

I thank Julia Penelope for her writing and her commitment to separatism; St. Louis activists Flowing Margaret Johnson and Laura Moore for their organizing and inspiration; and old friends for discussions about lesbian politics, especially Anne Waters, Chris Guerrero, Magda Mueller, Sorca O'Connor, Sue Lynn, Susan Echo, and Tineke Ritmeester.

Finally, I thank Janet Crites for her unfailing love and support.

Some of the writings in *Dyke Ideas* appear in print for the first time in this volume; others are revised or rewritten versions of pieces that have appeared elsewhere, as follows:

"Notes on the Meaning of Life" is a revision of an essay that appeared in *Lesbian Ethics* 1, no. 1 (Fall 1984), 90-94.

"Craziness" is based on two published writings: "Craziness and the Concept of Rape" in *WomanSpirit* 9, no. 34 (Winter Solstice 1982), 28-30, (a correction appeared in *WomanSpirit* 10, no. 37 [Fall Equinox 1983], 44); and "Craziness as a Source of Separatism" in *For Lesbians Only: A Separatist Anthology*, edited by Sarah Lucia Hoagland and Julia Penelope (London: Onlywomen Press, 1988), 196-99.

"Guilt," "Stalking Guilt," and "Story" appeared in *Lesbian Ethics* 5, no. 1 (Summer 1993), 72-75.

An earlier version of "Dyke Methods" was published as "Dyke Methods, or Principles for the Discovery/Creation of the Withstanding" in *Hypatia: A Journal of Feminist Philosophy* 3, no. 2 (Summer 1988), 1-13. This essay also appeared in *Hag Rag*, in two parts: Part I, *Hag Rag* 3, no. 4 (January-February 9989), 4-7, and *Hag Rag* 3, no. 5 (March-April 9989), 8-11. I added to the discussion in "Dyke Methods in Process," *Hag Rag* 4, no. 3 (May-June 9989), 8-9, and "More Dyke Methods,"

Hypatia 5, no. 1 (Spring 1990), 140-144. A revised version of the original essay was published in the anthology *Lesbian Philosophies and Cultures*, edited by Jeffner Allen (Albany, N.Y.: State University of New York Press, 1990), 15-29.

"Methods in Ethics" appeared in the anthology *Feminist Ethics*, edited by Claudia Card (Lawrence, Kansas: University Press of Kansas, 1991), 45-51.

"Not Lesbian Philosophy" was originally written for the Lesbian Philosophy issue of *Hypatia* that Claudia Card edited: *Hypatia: A Journal of Feminist Philosophy* 7, no. 4, (Fall 1992).

"Taking Responsibility for Sexuality" was written for a conference and so appeared first in *Women and Mental Health: Conference Proceedings*, edited by Elaine Barton, Kristen Watts-Penny, and Barbara Hillyer Davis (Norman, Oklahoma: University of Oklahoma Women's Studies Program, 1982), 55-62. A slightly revised version was later published as a pamphlet by Acacia Books (Berkeley, Calif.: 1983) and reprinted in *Philosophy and Sex*, second edition, edited by Robert Baker and Frederick Elliston (Buffalo, N.Y.: Prometheus Books, 1984), 421-30.

A brief piece entitled "Decentering Sex," from which I developed the essay of that title that is included here, was in the St. Louis lesbian periodical *LesTalk* 2, no. 4 (December 1992), 20.